THE
COMPLETE BOOK
OF
DOG
CARE

THE
COMPLETE BOOK
OF
DOG
CARE

JANE OLIVER

∥ ·PARRAGON· ∥

Picture credits

(Abbreviations key: R = Right, L = Left, T = Top, C = Centre, B = Below, A = Above))

ARDEA, LONDON : 76; /John Daniels: 4, 12BL, 12TR, 19, 44, 72; /Jean-Paul Ferrero: 6, 14B, 29, 60, 61, 71
Bruce Colman Ltd: 33T, 64, 74; /Mark Boulton: 34; /Thomas Buchholz: 40; /Jane Burton: 11, 18, 25, 27, 32T, 36, 45, 47, 48T, 49, 52B, 58, 70, 84, 93; /Eric
Crichton: 10, 42; /Bob Glover: 57; /Dr. Rocco Longo: 82; /Fritz Prenzel: 12TL; /Hans Reinhard: 7, 8, 9, 13, 14T, 31, 48B, 52T, 54, 73; /Kim Taylor: 15;
/John Topham: 38; Gunter Ziesler: 43
Marc Henrie: 20, 21, 23, 32B, 66
The Photographers' Library: 35, 41, 78, 95
Spectrum Colour Library: 22, 30, 33B, 39, 50, 68, 69, 81; /D.E. Lennon: 67
ZEFA: 17, 24, 75, 79, 86

Every effort has been made to trace the copyright holders and we apologize in advance for any unintentional omissions. We would be pleased to insert
the appropriate acknolwedgement in any subsequent edition of this publication.

Cover pictures
TL: Bruce Coleman Ltd/John Cancalosi
ACL: Bruce Coleman Ltd/Hans Reinhard
BCL: Bruce Coleman Ltd/Dr. Rocco Longo
BL: Bruce Coleman Ltd/Bob Glover
BC: ARDEA, LONDON/J.M. Labat
TR: Bruce Coleman Ltd/ Hans Reinhard
ACR: Bruce Coleman Ltd/Hans Reinhard
BCR: Bruce Coleman Ltd/Fritz Prenzel
BR: ARDEA, LONDON/John- Paul Ferrero
Front flap: ARDEA, LONDON/ John Daniels
Back flap: Bruce Coleman Ltd/Steven C. Kaufman

First published in 1994 by
Parragon Book Service Ltd
4 Mulberry Close
Rosslyn Hill
Hampstead
London
NW3 5UP

Designer: Sue Michniewicz
Line Illustrations: Pond and Giles
Editor: Alexa Stace

ISBN 1 85813 424 2

Printed in Italy

CONTENTS

Chapter 1
MAKING THE RIGHT CHOICE

Once a dog joins your household it will be part of the family for the

next 15 years or more, so it is important to consider what you

and the dog need from one another.

You may want a companion, a protector and a playmate for the children, or you may have ambitions for a dog as a competitor in obedience trials or the show ring. Your reasons for wanting a dog as a pet will make a considerable difference to the type of dog you choose, but whether the dog you select is large or small, pedigree or mongrel, dignified or sporting, it will demand a great deal from you in terms of time, attention and care. Cuddly puppies can grow up into energetic, hungry and wilful adults so before you take the plunge, make certain that you have room for a dog in your life and remember that a dog's loyalty and devotion will repay all the time and money you spend many times over.

THE RIGHT DOG FOR YOU

Dogs come in all shapes and sizes and it is essential to choose a shape and size that suits your home and lifestyle. Thousands of

ABOVE: *Working dogs like this rottweiler need careful handling to school their strength and abilities in the right direction.*

OPPOSITE: *It is essential to choose a breed that suits your home and lifestyle. These beautiful Afghans, for example, require a regular commitment to grooming.*

dogs are discarded every year by owners who fall for an elegant outline or a handsome coat, without giving a thought to the hours that must be spent on exercising and grooming. A well-

publicized win by an Afghan or an Old English Sheepdog at a major show can result in hundreds of unwanted pets up for adoption over the next 18 months.

First consider the size and type of your home. It would be unkind to confine a Great Dane or an Irish Wolfhound to a small flat; they need plenty of living space. If you live at the top of three flights of stairs remember that you might have to carry down a sick or convalescent animal two or three times a day for

BELOW: *Pekingese* (left) *and Papillon make delightful companions and require less exercise than larger breeds.*

ABOVE: *The diminutive size of the chihuahua makes it a popular addition to households with little space.*

DOG COSTS

Over its lifetime, your dog will cost you some thousands of pounds, so it is wise to estimate for the essentials in advance. Take into account:

* Initial outlay: bed, indoor or outdoor kennel, food bowls, toys, collar and lead.

* Food: the larger the dog, the bigger the food bill.

* Neutering: more expensive for females than males.

* Vaccinations and annual boosters.

* Veterinary bills for illness: an unknown quantity.

* Professional clipping and grooming.

* Training and obedience classes.

* Extra fencing needed to keep your dog on your property: this must always be well maintained.

* Damage replacements: puppies or destructive adult dogs can add quite a bit to household costs.

toilet requirements and an extra few kilos could injure you for life! Then think about where and how you will exercise your dog. If the only available exercise is round a city block, then a Retriever, Setter or Greyhound would be an unsuitable choice, however much you admire their looks. Consider how much time you can devote to training a dog; if your life is too busy to allow the time necessary, you should not take on strong, potentially fierce dogs - Rottweiler, German Shepherd, Dobermann - that need firm handling and careful training. Last but not least, think about the cost: a large dog will be considerably more expensive than a small one.

Puppies are very appealing but they really need a household where someone will be at home most of the day. However cute they look, they will go through a wet and messy stage, followed by a teething stage when they chew everything in sight. The great advantage is that you should be able to train your puppy to your own ways, while an adult dog will have formed its character and may have deeply ingrained bad habits. Most dogs can be re-educated, but this will take time and patience.

Bitches often have a gentler temperament than male dogs and they can be easier to train and less likely to wander, but they will come 'on heat' twice a year. This means a messy, blood-stained discharge, a bitch determined to escape and find a mate and all the dogs of the neighbourhood gathered at your door. Males may be more aggressive and headstrong, so that they need a firmer hand from the owner, though in some breeds there are no noticeable differences between the sexes. Either sex can be neutered, though this operation is most often performed on bitches. It can be the answer to some behaviour problems in males, such as wandering, aggression and scent marking around the house, but many owners prefer to avoid it, believing that the character of the dog often changes, so that it becomes lazier and less protective.

A mongrel, with an array of mixed breeds in its past history, will be much cheaper at the outset than a pedigree dog, although it will not necessarily be any cheaper to keep. Although you can see a mongrel's mother, the other partner in the mating may be a mystery and the puppies may grow up looking nothing like her. Whereas with a pure-bred dog you will know its future size, general appearance and likely temperament, this will all be pot luck in a mongrel. On the other hand, mongrels do not suffer from the hereditary and congenital defects found in particular breeds. If you have the opportunity of buying a cross-breed dog - the offspring of two pure-bred parents of different breeds – this may be a good choice, as cross-breeds often have the good attributes of both parents.

WHICH BREED?

Even if you have a good idea of the dog you want, take the trouble to read one of the many books outlining the characteristics and temperament of each breed, in case there is something you have overlooked. You can see the various breeds going through their paces at dog shows and most owners will be only too pleased to tell you all about their favoured breed – though they are likely to be biased! Any further information can be obtained from breed clubs, which can be contacted through the Kennel Club in each country. Before you make your final choice of breed, check with your veterinarian whether it is liable to suffer from hereditary defects such as deformed hip joints (German Shepherd, American Cocker Spaniel and English Setter, among others), progressive retinal atrophy which leads to blindness (Golden and Labrador Retrievers, Pekingese, Poodle and Welsh Corgi, among others) or deafness (Great Dane, Bull Terrier and Dachshund, among others).

Generalizations about breeds are full of pitfalls but the various groups recognized by Kennel Clubs do share various characteristics.

GUNDOGS: friendly, with pleasing temperaments, they make good family dogs but not-so-good guard dogs. They have lots of energy and need plenty of exercise.

HOUNDS: hardy, independent hunters but most make good companions and adapt well as house dogs.

UTILITY DOGS: (called 'non-sporting' in the U.S.): these include such diverse breeds as Dalmatians, Bulldogs, Shih Tzu, and Lhasa Apso. They are lively with attractive personalities and are good barkers so many of them make useful guard dogs, in addition to the more obvious breeds.

WORKING DOGS: include guard dogs and herding dogs like Collies, Dobermann, German Shepherds and Rottweilers and

BELOW: *Good-natured and affectionate, basset hounds are irresistible, especially at this age.*

ABOVE: *Mongrels make ideal pets and have the advantage that they do not suffer from the hereditary and congenital defects found in many breeds.*

they need the right handling to school their strength and abilities in the right direction. They are loyal and devoted with a highly developed protective streak.

TERRIERS: friendly, alert and fast-moving, they make good pets and protectors but they can be excitable and yappy.

TOY DOGS: happy, self-confident little dogs with more courage than size. They make delightful companions and are a good choice for the elderly, or those who are unable to give their dogs much exercise.

WHERE TO FIND YOUR PEDIGREE DOG

Obviously, a reputable breeder is the best source and if you are looking for a popular breed, one of the local veterinarians may be able to put you in touch. Breeders advertise in dog magazines and will often be represented at dog shows. If you have any difficulty in finding your chosen breed, obtain the address of the appropriate breed society from the Kennel Club.

Buying from a pet shop is probably the least satisfactory method of obtaining a puppy. However lovingly they are cared for, they have been put under a great deal of stress in being taken from their mothers and then housed in cramped conditions with other animals and the excitement of a constant procession of strangers. The transmission of disease is far more likely when dogs from different homes are housed together and stressed animals are more vulnerable to infection.

ABOVE LEFT: *King Charles spaniels are generally reliable with children and make good, loyal companions.*

ABOVE : *Boxers require a fair amount of exercise and they are good with children making them excellent family pets.*

LEFT: *Their striking black and white 'spotted' colouring endears dalmatians to many people. They also make excellent guard dogs.*

Some breeders have older puppies or ex-show dogs for sale – often dogs that have not lived up to their early potential. If these dogs have been reared as house pets, they may be a good buy but if they have always lived in kennels, they may never make good pets.

Many adult pure-bred dogs are in need of good homes for a variety of sound reasons - family break-up, an emigrating

GOOD LOYAL COMPANIONS	GOOD WITH CHILDREN	GOOD GUARDS	GOOD FOR TRAINING
Affenpinscher	Basenji	Bouvier des Flandres	Australian Cattle Dog
Border Terrier	Border Terrier	Bullmastiff	Border Collie
Boxer	Boxer	Dalmatian	Dobermann
Collie	Bull Terrier	Dobermann	German Shepherd
Dachshund	English Setter	German Shepherd	Golden Retriever
English Terrier	Labrador Retriever	Great Dane	Labrador
Fox Terrier	Staffordshire Bull Terrier	Old English Sheepdog	Poodle
Irish Terrier	Siberian Husky	Rottweiler	Schnauzer
Irish Wolfhound		Schipperke	Weimaraner
King Charles Spaniel		Welsh Corgi	
Pug			

owner, an allergic child – and you may find your ideal dog through an advertisement in the local paper. There are rescue societies for most breeds and, once again, you can obtain details through the Kennel Club. In Britain the address is 1–5 Clarges Street, London W1Y 8AB.

If you are interested in an adult dog and you are able to talk to the previous owner, or obtain a full history from a breed rescue society, try asking the following questions:

How old is the dog?
How many owners has it had?
Who is the usual veterinarian and how many veterinary visits has the dog made in the previous year?
Are its inoculations up to date?
Is it used to other pets?
Is it used to children?
Does it have any bad habits; is it destructive or aggressive towards people or other dogs, does it bark excessively?
What commands does it respond to?
What type of discipline has been used in the past?
Why is a new home necessary?

RIGHT: *This hunting dog enjoys an active outdoor lifestyle and responds well to training.*

Answers may or may not be forthcoming and in any case, you will have to judge the truth of them for yourself, but many owners are very distressed at a necessary parting and will be anxious to cooperate in making the transition as painless as possible for the dog.

WHERE TO FIND YOUR MONGREL

Anyone with a mongrel litter to home will welcome you with open arms – just tell your friends that you are in the market and ask them to spread the word. You could also ask at the local dog-training class and at nearby schools, where a teacher might be willing to make inquiries or put up a notice asking anyone

LEFT: *The alsatian or German shepherd is classed as a working dog. It is very active and makes a reliable guard dog.*

BELOW: *Shaggiest of the shaggy dogs, the Pyrennean shepherd has an insatiable appetite for walks.*

with puppies for sale to contact you. Ask around among neighbourhood veterinarians too; they may well know of bitches with unplanned pregnancies.

ABOVE: *A young border collie, just 21 weeks old, is already brimful of strength and energy.*

Veterinarians are also a good source for obtaining an older dog as they often have healthy dogs brought in for euthanasia because their owners can no longer keep them. Caring owners in difficulties over keeping a pet are just as likely to advertise for a new home for a mongrel as for a pedigree dog and in this case you ask all the questions listed above.

Animal shelters and welfare societies always have plenty of dogs (pedigree *and* mongrel) waiting for adoption and you will find them very hard to resist as they wag their tails and gaze up at you hopefully. Before you make a choice, do talk to the staff about the dog. Some of the dogs in shelters have a history of bad treatment by cruel or insensitive owners, others have behaviour problems that mean they have been returned by adopters once or twice already. If you are an experienced dog owner and have unlimited patience, you may be able to take on such a dog, but you must be aware of the problems ahead. When you find a dog you like, take it out of the pen and see how it reacts to you: does it come forward in a friendly and curious manner, or is it wary and apt to cringe? Examine its head and its body, noticing if it flinches away from you at any point. Hold each paw briefly and see if the dog accepts this without anxiety. If possible, play a game with the dog: is it apa-

thetic or does it get over-excited? Are you sure that you can cope with the dog's strength?

Representatives of welfare societies will want to interview you before letting you take a dog and they may want to visit your home. You should not resent this; they want to be sure that the adoption will be successful, as a rejected dog will be that much more difficult to house next time. It is important that you make a donation – as generous as you can manage – to enable the organization to help other animals.

PICK OF THE LITTER

Always choose your puppy in person, even if it means travelling a long distance to see the litter. However sure you are of the breeder and the dog's pedigree, 'mail order' is not the right way to acquire an animal. Tell the breeder that you will want to see the whole litter, with the mother. This means that you can check on the health and temperament of the bitch and observe the behaviour of the puppies with their littermates. You are entitled to be suspicious of any breeder who will not allow this.

EXAMINING A PUPPY

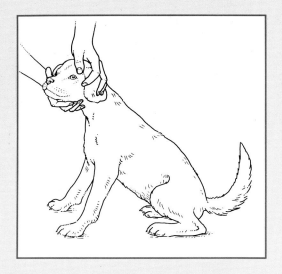

THE EYES should be bright and clear, with no discharge and no sign of inflammation.

THE MOUTH should be odour-free, with pink gums and teeth that clench well.

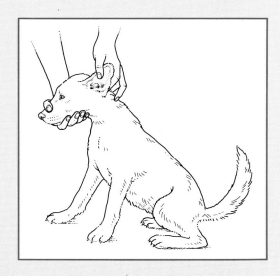

THE EARS should be clean inside with no sign of discharge and odour-free. The hairs around the edge should be clean.

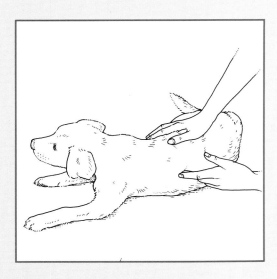

THE COAT should be shiny and clean with no bare patches or scales and no black specks that could indicate flea infestation.

If you have answered an advertisement, beware of unscrupulous dealers who buy in litters cheaply and sell them at a profit. If you find several assorted litters on the premises, with no mothers in evidence, do not buy. Such dealers often pay little attention to the health of the dogs and the puppies may already be diseased.

When you visit, take notice of the cleanliness of the surroundings, and whether the pups have been brought up so far as part of the family or in isolation. The most important time for the puppy's 'socialization' is between 6 and 13 weeks and if you are taking it home at 8 weeks, when it is fully weaned, its previous experiences will be important for future development.

EXAMINING A PUPPY CONT.

THE ANAL AREA should be clean and dry with no sign of discharge or diarrhoea.

THE BODY should have a moderate layer of fat under the skin and the skin should be loose and pliable. If the ribs feel bony but the skin is stretched tight over the abdomen, the puppy may have worms. A swelling on the tummy or in the groin could mean a hernia.

Spend time making your choice: never rush. The puppies should be active and inquisitive, eager to jump up and investigate when a new face appears. Look for any signs of lameness or unsociability - a pup that shows no interest or backs away while others surge forward will probably not make a good pet. Avoid the bossy, over-pushy puppy, but choose one that will allow itself to be handled without whining or growling. When you pick it up, the puppy should be relaxed and feel heavier, not lighter, than you expect.

RIGHT: *Chosen from an animal shelter, this happy dog is introduced to its new family.*

Chapter 2
THE NEW ARRIVAL

When a puppy arrives in your house, it will have no idea what you expect of it.

It is separated from its mother and littermates for the first time and everything that

happens is exciting, bewildering and frightening by turns.

If you are patient and consistent, the puppy will soon learn your house rules, but don't expect too much too quickly. A mature dog will need just as much patience – more if it has had bad experiences in the past – as it will have built up behaviour patterns that may not fit into its new life. Think of this as the canine equivalent of being in a foreign country with people who speak an unfamiliar language, and give it time.

ESSENTIAL EQUIPMENT

BEDS The puppy's first bed can be a cardboard box lined with newspaper and old sweaters. This will provide a comfortable resting place and surround it with the smells of its new family –

OPPOSITE: *This three-week-old puppy is a blue schipperke, also known as a Belgian or Dutch barge dog.*

RIGHT: *It is unusual for families to acquire more than one puppy from a litter, and separation from its littermates is one of the major adjustments a newly acquired puppy must make.*

the box can be changed as often as necessary, as needle-sharp teeth shred its sides. Put the box in a quiet, draught-free corner which can become the dog's retreat and refuge. As the pup grows past the teething stage it can graduate to one of the many styles of bed available. Beanbags filled with polystyrene granules, with washable outer covers, provide a cosy nest, plastic beds lined with washable mattresses are durable and chew-proof and small dogs can cuddle into the 'igloo' beds usually meant for cats. Wicker beds look attractive and dogs like their comfortable creaking sounds, but they are good for chewing and pieces could be swallowed by mistake. Any bed should be big enough to allow the dog to stretch out and to turn round and round before settling down.

FOOD BOWLS Choose food bowls that will enable the dog to eat without trailing its ears in the food: for breeds with long, pendulous ears this means a bowl with fairly tall sides that slope inwards at the top. Stainless steel bowls with a rubber rim underneath so that they do not slide around the floor are easy to keep clean and well worth the extra cost. Plastic and aluminium dishes are easily overturned and you will probably find a heavy

pottery bowl most suitable for water. Keep a special knife and fork for the dog's food and wash all utensils separately from the family dishes.

INDOOR KENNELS Many owners find an indoor kennel or training pen an invaluable aid to managing a new puppy. These are obtainable from larger pet shops and usually consist of individual wire mesh panels which clip together. The pen should be high enough to allow the dog to stand up comfortably (if you want the pen to last beyond puppyhood, then take into account how large your dog is likely to grow) and wide enough to allow it to stretch right out. A pen might look like a prison to you but, properly used, it will be a safe den for your dog, protected from running feet and boisterous pets. From the owner's point of view, it means far less time and worry protecting your puppy from household hazards - and

BELOW: *Extending leashes give a dog more freedom while still leaving the owner in control.*

protecting your furniture from your puppy's teeth. Unfortunately pens are expensive but DIY enthusiasts may be able to construct a cheaper alternative or, for a puppy, a child's playpen may be adequate.

COLLARS AND LEASHES A leather leash looks handsome when new but will need oiling to keep it in good condition. Nylon leashes are cheaper, easy to wash and fold into your pocket but are probably not suitable for a large, heavy dog. Extending leashes give a dog more freedom while still leaving the owner in control.

For a collar, woven nylon is more lasting than leather and should be fitted carefully so that it will not come over the dog's head when it pulls backwards but is loose enough for you to slip two fingers between collar and neck. Puppies grow quickly so test the collar frequently and buy a larger size as soon as necessary. The width of the collar should vary according to the size of the dog; up to 50mm (2in) for large dogs, 25mm (1in) for medium size and 12mm (½ in) for the toy breeds, though with these tiny dogs a light harness which fits over the head and round the chest may be a better idea.

The check-chain or 'choke-chain' enjoyed widespread popularity a few years back and is still widely used among trainers. This is a chain collar worn for training sessions only. It lies loose around the dog's neck but at a tug on the leash it tightens immediately and uncomfortably, checking any undesirable movement the dog is making. More recently, a number of

ABOVE: *A golden retriever displays a head halter, which is designed to give the owner more control over a very strong or difficult dog.*

experts have come out against the use of the check chain, pointing out that it can easily cause injury to the dog when wrongly used and, also, that it is unnecessarily harsh. A gentler method of controlling a strong or difficult dog is a head halter, made from strong nylon, which enables the owner to steer the dog in much the same way as a stable-hand can steer a horse.

In many countries, including Britain, you are required by law to see that your dog wears some form of identification at all times.

PUPPY TIPS

* With a new puppy in the house keep outside doors locked and windows closed.

* Keep breakables out of reach and unplug electrical items in case the puppy chews the flex.

* Keep the puppy indoors until it is fully protected by vaccination.

* Don't smack your puppy if it makes mistakes; it will probably be thoroughly bewildered and it may come to fear you.

* Make sure your puppy has plenty of company; it should not be left alone for long periods or shut away from the rest of the family.

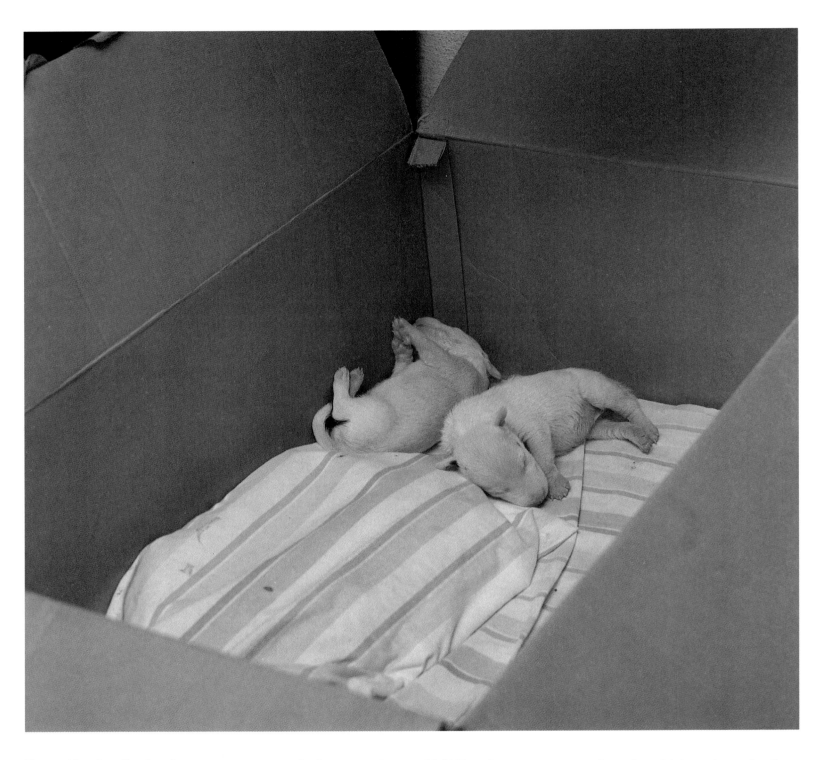

Fit an identity disc bearing your surname, telephone number and, perhaps, the number of your veterinarian. Omit the dog's name, as someone might use it to lure your dog away.

ABOVE: *Bull terrier puppies enjoy the comforts of their new home. A well-wrapped hot water bottle replaces the warmth of their mother and littermates.*

THE FIRST DAYS

Arrange to collect your dog at a time when there will be someone at home most of the day for at least the first week (longer in the case of a puppy). Don't schedule it for shortly before you go on holiday, with all the disruption that entails, or just before a major family celebration, with lots of extra people about and everyone rushed and over-excited. This will be both bewildering and over-stimulating for the dog and disastrous for any training routine you are trying to establish.

Check the puppy's normal diet with the breeder and plan to feed the same food at first, making any changes gradually. Collect the puppy by car if possible, and have a cardboard box lined with a blanket in the back. If you are driving, take a helper with you, so that there is someone to talk to the puppy and play with it. If it cannot see the countryside whizzing by and has something to do, it is less likely to be car sick and associate car journeys with unpleasant feelings.

If you have to travel by public transport, you should use a secure carrier; it is far too risky to carry a puppy inside your coat. A cat owner might lend you a suitable carrier of the type that can be thoroughly washed afterwards, or you can buy a cardboard carrying case quite cheaply. Line it with a plastic sheet and plenty of newspaper and support it underneath, not just by the handle. If the puppy vomits or urinates during the journey, the carrier will be weakened.

When you get home, take the puppy outside, to the area of the garden where you will want it to eliminate regularly and stay with it there for a few minutes. If it performs, praise it effusively. Then take it indoors and keep it in one room for the time being. *Stay with it*; a new puppy will become very distressed if it is shut away alone. Shortly after arrival, offer a small meal. Once it has eaten, take it outside again if it did not perform before. Then let it settle down for a sleep.

There is no point in expecting a small puppy to sleep right through the night. It will need to relieve itself after a few hours and if you shut it up alone it may well howl disconsolately. If you do shut it up downstairs, put a warm hot water bottle, well-wrapped (stone is safer from sharp teeth than rubber) in its bed to replace the warmth of its mother and littermates. Set your alarm clock so that you get up a couple of times in the night to reassure your puppy and take it out for a few minutes. The puppy will probably be far less anxious if it can settle down in a pen in your bedroom, but be sure to protect the carpet with plenty of newspaper, in case of accidents. Otherwise, forget all the strictures about 'starting how you mean to go on' and take the puppy to bed with you. Having a dog sharing your bed permanently is not very hygienic but it will be very comforting for an anxious puppy for two or three nights, while it becomes accustomed to its new home. It will adapt much more easily to overnight separation when this first traumatic stage has passed.

If you have adopted an adult dog, let it settle into the household without fuss. Keep it with you all the time but don't make it the centre of attention. Go about all your normal tasks, but bolster its confidence with a 'good, good dog' now and again, so that it knows it is accepted. Keep the atmosphere calm and make no sudden movements; let the dog come to you in its own good time.

BELOW: *Never carry a puppy in your arms for long distances. A secure carrier will ensure your new puppy reaches home safely during this unpredictable stage.*

INTRODUCTIONS ALL ROUND

Let your puppy meet the rest of the family one at a time, in peaceful surroundings. Children must understand that squeezing, teasing and pulling at ears, tail or fur are not allowed and that play must be limited at first - after half an hour of play, a puppy needs to sleep. All contact between children and dogs should be supervised until you are quite certain that they can be trusted together. Children can provoke dogs beyond all reason, without realizing that they are doing anything wrong, and cannot read the danger signals if the dog is losing control.

An adopted dog should have been chosen carefully for its good relations with children but even so, introductions should be made with care. If children understand that the dog must be allowed to make the first approach and that they should then extend a hand, palm down and fingers curled inwards so that the dog can sniff it, before they stroke its neck and shoulders, then all should be well. Older children can be encouraged to feed and walk the dog, so that it becomes a real family pet. However, it is irresponsible to entrust a dog to a child who is not strong enough to control it fully.

The family cat will have no trouble at all putting an upstart puppy in its place, but it is wise to trim the cat's claws before they meet; otherwise your new puppy might end up with a badly scratched nose. An adult dog should be introduced on a leash and it must learn quickly – and consistently – that no chasing is allowed. The cat will feel more secure if there is a nearby shelf or other high place where it can take refuge if necessary. A dog, of whatever age, should not be left alone with a cat until they are firmly established friends or, at the very least, have learned to ignore one another.

The first meeting between an established dog and a puppy should take place in the garden. Have the dog on a leash and talk to it and fuss it while someone else brings out the puppy. Keep concentrating on your dog and pay no attention to the puppy. If, when they have done all the preliminary sniffing, there are no signs of hostility, then let the dog off the leash and call it to follow you indoors. The puppy will follow along and your dog will feel that it is leading the youngster into the house. Stop any signs of aggression immediately and always praise any friendly overtures but supervise all contact unless the puppy is protected in a pen.

ABOVE: *Animals need introductions as well as humans.*

LEFT: *Meeting the family, one at a time.*

LIFTING A DOG

There may be times when you need to carry your dog, however large it may be, so it is wise to get the dog used to being lifted and held from the beginning. If your dog is already an adult and nervous about being picked up at first, it may help if another family member talks reassuringly to the dog and strokes its head. It will soon get used to the idea and if it feels itself supported firmly and confidently, there should be no problems.

A small dog or a puppy can be lifted in the same way as a cat, with one hand under its chest and the other under its behind. Never try to pick up a puppy the way its mother does, by the scruff of the neck. With a larger dog, hold it with one arm under its chest in front of the forelegs and the other under its behind and round the hind legs. Don't bend from the waist - that's the quick way to a damaged back. Instead, bend your knees and draw the dog up to your chest.

Lift a large dog with one arm beneath its chest and the other around its hind legs.

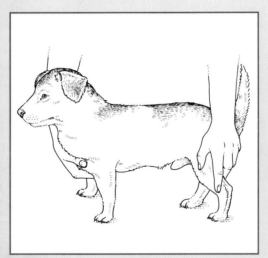

Lift a small dog with one hand under its chest and the other beneath its behind.

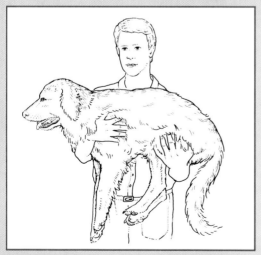

When you lift, bend your knees and draw the dog to your chest.

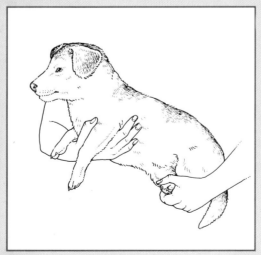

Lift the dog towards your chest for carrying.

HOUSETRAINING

Your puppy will have little bowel or bladder control at first and you need to accept that there will be a few unavoidable accidents before training is complete. Just how many accidents you can prevent depends on how good you are at predicting your dog's needs. It will probably need to 'go' soon after waking, eating or a bout of vigorous activity, so take it out at these times. At any other time, you may see the puppy pawing the ground, sniffing round or turning in a circle. When this happens, act quickly to get the puppy outside.

If possible, choose a place in the garden where there is some rough grass. Dogs seem to prefer their toilet to be on grass, but if you choose a corner of the lawn, it will soon develop brown patches. Always stay with the puppy in the garden so that you can tell it how well it has done when it performs on schedule. If you shut it out, it will think about nothing but getting in again. Reckon on making half a dozen trips a day and when you make the last evening trip, see that the puppy has a vigorous run round the garden, as exercise will stimulate the bladder and bowels.

Some owners prefer paper-training the puppy, which means that you will not have to spend so much time standing out in the garden. You will need to confine the puppy to one easily cleaned room - probably the kitchen, with an outside door - and cover the floor with several layers of newspaper. The puppy will probably pick one area and return to it again and again. Once this happens, remove the paper from the rest of the floor, leaving a single toilet area. Move this gradually towards the door, then leave the door open and place the newspaper outside. Once the routine is well-established, you will be able to dispense with the paper. The disadvantage with this method is that it does teach the puppy to eliminate indoors, which it then has to un-learn.

Do not punish your puppy for a mistake, any more than you would punish your baby before it is potty-trained. If you catch it in the act you can say 'No!' firmly, but shouting or rubbing its nose in the mess will be counter-productive. It may make the puppy nervous and more likely to urinate in the wrong place, or it may teach it not to eliminate in front of you, so that it hides away at the crucial moment. You may find a pen useful as an aid to house-training. A dog's instincts will tell it not to foul its sleeping area so the puppy will probably become restless and begin to whine when it needs to go out.

ABOVE: *The first meeting between an established dog and a new puppy should take place under supervision in the garden.*

HOUSETRAINING WITH THE PAPER METHOD

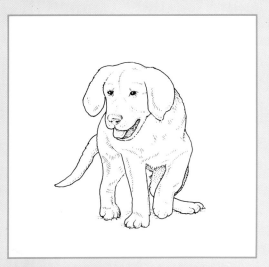

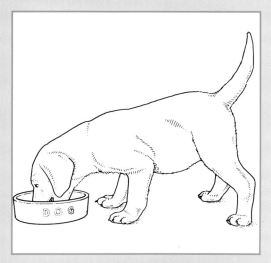

1 Your puppy will probably need to 'go' soon after a meal.

2 The puppy will soon get used to heading for the corner of the room where the paper is laid.

3 The puppy performs as required in the correct place.

4 Praise the puppy and gradually move the toilet area towards and then out the door.

VACCINATIONS

Puppies are protected from infection by the colostrum in their mother's milk for some weeks after birth but it is essential that by eight weeks or so your puppy is vaccinated against the major infectious diseases: canine distemper or 'hardpad' (a virus that can lead to serious complications in the nervous system), infectious canine hepatitis or Rubarth's disease (a virus affecting the liver), parvovirus (a relatively new virus that affects the intestines and can affect the heart muscle) and leptospirosis (a bacterial disease affecting the liver or kidneys). Vaccination is no absolute guarantee that your dog will be protected but in the unlikely event that it does catch one of the diseases, it should be far less severe than in an unvaccinated animal.

The routine suggested by your veterinarian will depend on the risks in your neighbourhood, but most give the first injection at eight weeks, and the second at 12 weeks. Some recommend a third injection at 16 weeks. After that, you should take your dog for an annual booster.

In North America and Europe rabies vaccinations are required by law, usually with a first injection at nine weeks and the second a year later, with regular boosters. In the U.K. strict quarantine laws are enforced to keep rabies out.

When you take your puppy for its injections, the veterinarian will give a general health check-up and also advise on routine worming. Puppies should be treated for roundworms on a monthly basis until they are about six months old and adults will need worming three times a year.

BELOW: *A patient and sensible approach to the arrival of a new puppy will reward you in years to come.*

Chapter 3
FOOD AND FEEDING

There is no difficulty about providing a balanced diet for your dog;

there are plenty of good proprietary foods on the market and, properly used,

they will keep your dog in peak condition.

The main problem for most owners is limiting diet to a healthy amount. In the wild, dogs will gorge themselves whenever food is available, eating all they can get because they do not know when their next meal is coming; many domestic dogs, even though well and regularly fed, will behave in the same way. They also became experts at wheedling tidbits and table scraps from their owners at every opportunity and this can lead to obesity and many attendant problems.

PUPPY FEED

When you bring your puppy home, keep to its accustomed diet for the time being. Any changes should be phased in little by little to cut the risk of tummy upsets. The gold rule for feeding puppies is little and often - though many of them eat a lot and often.

ABOVE: *Avoid feeding puppies from the larger breeds, like this Bernese mountain dog, excessive quantities in the hope that they will attain maturity more quickly.*

OPPOSITE: *The golden rule for puppy feeding is little and often.*

31

Until four months, puppies should have four meals a day, the first and third meal usually being baby cereal or puppy meal soaked in milk and the second and fourth being meat meals – canned puppy food or mince mixed with bread or puppy biscuits. You will see, from the way your puppy looks, how much it needs: if it looks rather lean, add more cereal and biscuits, but if it is looking podgy, cut down on the carbohydrates. After four months, cut out the first meal and increase the quantity of food at other meals. At six or seven months, cut out the other milk and cereal meal and from about nine months you can, if you wish, feed a single meal a day.

If you have chosen one of the giant breeds, don't make the mistake of feeding giant meals so that it will attain its full height as quickly as possible. If its bones grow too quickly, they will not have the necessary strength, so steady growth is better for its future health.

Puppies tend to chew anything that comes their way, so they ingest all sorts of rubbish and normally they seem to come to no harm. Occasional slight diarrhoea is nothing to worry about but if it persists, and the puppy seems bright and healthy otherwise, try cutting the amount of milk in the diet. If the puppy seems unwell, consult your veterinarian without delay.

ABOVE: *A border collie puppy is bottle-fed with a special milk substitute available from pet shops.*

BELOW: *A day-old puppy is totally reliant on its mother for survival.*

LEFT: *A golden retriever has been taught to beg for a tasty treat.*

HAND-REARING A PUPPY

If a bitch dies, rejects a pup or is unable to provide enough milk, the best answer is to find a foster-mother and veterinarians or animal shelters may be able to help. If this is not possible, you are faced with hand-rearing one or more puppies and this is a very demanding, time-consuming job.

At first the puppy should be kept at a temperature of 29.5°C (85°F), which can be reduced to 24°C (75°F) by four weeks. Use a heat pad in the puppy's bed as well as a warm hot-water bottle, well-wrapped, but leave a cooler area where the puppy can move if necessary. You can supplement the room heat with an infra-red lamp, placed well out of the puppy's reach, but check temperatures with a thermometer to make sure it is not too hot.

Feed at first two-hourly and after a couple of days three-hourly between 6am and midnight, with another couple of meals in the night for the first two weeks. Then space out feeds a little more. Use a special milk substitute, obtainable from pet shops.

BELOW: *Pembroke corgis feed from their own saucers. Never allow your dog to lick your own plate clean after a meal.*

FEEDING DO'S AND DONT'S

* Do make sure that clean water is always available.

* Don't feed your dog on cat food; its protein content is too high.

* Do serve food at room temperature, not straight from the refrigerator.

* Don't expect your dog to live on table scraps; our food is highly processed and will not contain all the necessary nutrients.

* Do add a little vegetable oil to the feed if your dog's coat is looking dull.

* Don't overfeed your dog; obesity will probably shorten its life.

Don't use cow's milk as it does not have sufficient nutrients. If possible, make up fresh formula for each feed, though a day's supply can be stored in the refrigerator. Your veterinarian will advise on the correct amount for your puppy. Warm the formula to blood heat, use a puppy feeding bottle and be patient: let the puppy feed in its own time. Sterilize the feeding equipment and be as careful about hygiene as you would be with a human baby, as the puppy will not have the protection from infection that its mother's milk would have given.

After each feed, wipe the puppy's mouth and then wipe the ano-genital area with cotton wool moistened with warm water. This mimics the action of the bitch in licking the puppy to stimulate it to pass urine and faeces.

At three weeks, give the puppy a little baby rice three or four times a day and offer some on your finger to encourage it to eat. Gradually begin adding a little freshly cooked meat.

THE ADULT DIET

Most dogs are fed once or twice a day, though toy dogs will need two or three small meals. You might find that when your dog is fed a single meal in the evening (particularly if it is canned food) it cannot get through the night without needing to relieve itself and if this is the case it is better to change to two meals. Some owners follow quite a different feeding regime, leaving dried food down all day so that the dog can eat what it wants, when it wants. The theory is that, though the dog eats more at first, in time it will regulate its intake. Unfortunately, no one has explained this theory to the dogs and a minority seem to go on scoffing indefinitely.

Your dog should eat only from its own bowl. Never put down your plate for the dog to lick clean and if you want to give it scraps from your food, keep them to supplement its next meal. Feeding your dog just before the family meal, or at the same time, will cut down the temptation to beg. If you keep two or more dogs, try not to feed them shoulder to shoulder. Less assertive dogs tend to get less than their share and the pushy dog may end up overweight. Also, you will not be able to tell if one animal is not eating properly because it is unwell.

BELOW: *Working dogs require a much greater food intake than, for example, a pet which takes a couple of short walks a day.*

GRASS-EATING

If your dog is eating grass constantly, it may be an indication of a gut infection, but some grass eating is perfectly normal and may be followed by vomiting. The grass acts as a useful emetic which rids the stomach of fur and bits of bone that might otherwise cause damage. It is important not to use garden fertilizers or herbicides which are harmful to pets.

Dogs are basically carnivores but they cannot live on meat alone. In the wild they would eat the whole of a small animal: flesh, bones and offal and pet dogs need a balanced diet containing protein, fat, carbohydrates, vitamins and minerals. Proprietary foods are manufactured to provide all the necessary nutrients but if you feed your dog on home-cooked food, you will have to take more care and make sure all the necessary elements are provided.

Types of food

Commercially prepared foods come in three main varieties:

CANNED FOOD: Some cans provide a 'complete' food, with cereal already added, while others need added meal to make up a balanced diet. Dogs who will not eat meat mixed with meal can be given biscuits instead, either with the meat or as tidbits, but be careful to ration them, so that you are not giving extra

carbohydrate treats all day long. Cans have a very long shelf-life but, once they are opened, the contents must be stored in the refrigerator and used as soon as possible.

SEMI-MOIST FOOD: This comes in foil sachets, each with an average serving, which can be stored without refrigeration before opening and they take up far less room in the cupboard than cans. Semi-moist food is relatively expensive but can be useful for fussy feeders, though it is unsuitable for diabetic dogs.

DRY FOOD: Usually in the form of flakes or pellets, dried food is a relatively low cost way of feeding your dog. It is particularly useful if you have to leave food down when you are out of the house, as it will not spoil. It can be stored for some weeks but will eventually lose its vitamin content, so keep an eye on the 'use by' date on the packet. Some dogs find dried food more palatable if it is mixed with water or gravy, but this means that it will spoil in the same way as canned food if it is left down for too long.

It is almost impossible to lay down rules for the amount your dog should eat: that will depend on its size, age and how much exercise it gets. Obviously a working dog will need much larger rations than a pet taking a couple of short walks a day. The following table is only a rough guide and you will need to judge for yourself the amount that enables your pet to keep healthy and lively without putting on weight.

	9kg (20lb) DOG	20kg (44lb) DOG	40kg (88lb) DOG
Canned food			
(2 parts)with biscuit	400g (14oz)	600g (21oz)	1100g (39oz)
(1 part) Semi-moist			
food	225g (8oz)	400g (14 oz)	650g (23 oz)
Dried food	180g (6oz)	300g (10 oz)	530g (18 oz)

If you are feeding your dog on home cooking, be sure to provide a good mix of meat with vegetables, some white fish and poultry as well as bread, rice and cereals. Feed offal only once or twice a week. All meat and fish should be cooked.

OPPOSITE: *However enticingly clean you keep a dog's waterbowl, there are times when a drink from the garden pond is much preferred.*

DRINKING

There is no set 'norm' for the amount of water a dog drinks in a day; in hot weather and after vigorous exercise consumption will increase and dogs on dry diets will drink more than those fed on canned food. However, it is a good idea to fill the water-bowl to the same level each day, then you know if your dog is drinking far more than usual. This may alert you to the early stages of a health problem.

Some dogs cannot digest milk and as it is not essential to a healthy diet, it is better to cut out milk altogether if it causes diarrhoea.

There is no harm in letting a dog that enjoys tea joining the family in an afternoon cup - although it is better not to add sugar - but don't let your pooch share your evening glass of beer. Dogs can become addicted to alcohol, just like humans, and some of the same problems will result.

THE VEGETARIAN DOG

Dogs can live a healthy life as vegetarians, as their bodies can convert vegetable protein and fat into the substances needed for all their bodily functions. A vegetarian diet can include soya protein, eggs, cheese, raw and cooked vegetables, fruit, wholegrain cereals and wholemeal bread. Raw carrots and cabbage stumps lightly roasted in the oven can provide them with something hard to chew, keeping their teeth in good condition and exercising their jaws. Vegetarian diets may be low in fat, so add a teaspoon of uncooked vegetable oil to the dog's food each day.

Getting the right balance of nutrients for dogs is more difficult in this type of diet, so ask your veterinarian about any necessary vitamin and mineral supplements. Remember that dogs will always eat meat if they can get it and, given the choice, your pet would be unlikely to pick vegetarianism. Vegetarian owners would do well to take a puppy rather than an adult dog, which will have to be retrained from its favourite eating habits.

FUSSY FEEDERS

Most dogs are not finicky eaters; they wolf down their food in a matter of minutes and don't seem to get bored with eating the same food at every meal. If your dog is picky, it may be because it is getting too many tidbits and it simply isn't very hungry at meal-times, so the first step is to cut out all between-meal snacks. Feed your dog one or two meals a day, not several, and cut down on the amount of fibre.

Warming the food to blood heat can encourage a dog to eat, especially if you then feed it beside the dining table when the rest of the family is eating. Toy breeds, in particular, are very good at manipulating their owners, rejecting their canned dog food because they know that something better will be offered to tempt them. The only answer is to be firm: put down the dish and leave it for, at most, an hour, then take it up again. Offer the same type of food at the next meal and follow the same procedure. Your dog will come to no harm if it misses a couple of meals and it will soon lose its fussy ways.

GREEDY DOGS

Fat dogs are not healthy dogs: obesity leads to heart disease, arthritis and diabetes and brings added risks if the dog needs an anaesthetic for surgery. Surveys show that nearly one-third of all dogs in the U.K. and America are overweight, with Spaniels, Retrievers, Labradors, Poodles, Dachshunds and Beagles among those most likely to add unwanted flab. Neutered dogs and bitches are most at risk, especially as they get older and less active.

Ideally, you should be able to feel, but not see, the dog's ribs. If you can see its sides bulging as it faces you head-on, then it is too fat. Begin the diet by cutting out all snacks between meals and keep a careful eye on the rest of the family to see that no one is providing secret feeds.

Putting a fat dog on an effective diet probably means cutting its food intake by about 40% for the time being. Feed several small meals instead of one large one and plan activities to involve and interest the dog before and after mealtimes. Distract the dog with toys and attention when it begs for food or follows you around looking accusing or soulful. Add bran to the food to help it feel full and provide plenty of strong rubber toys for chewing.

ELDERLY DOGS

Elderly dogs often need less food as their metabolism slows down. They need less protein but what they have should be of high quality, so replace some of the meat content of the diet with milk (unless it causes diarrhoea), egg, cheese or beef

extract. Fish and poultry may be more easily digested than meat and you may find that a dog formerly fed on dried food may now prefer canned food, which slips down easily. Feed two or three small meals instead of one large one and, if the dog is constipated, add a little bran.

BONES

Bones are not essential for a dog's wellbeing and though on the whole they are good for teeth, helping to keep them clean, they can sometimes cause teeth to fracture. If you have the sort of dog that always tries to crack bones instead of gnawing at them they are better avoided. In any case, never give poultry bones as these splinter and can become stuck in the mouth or throat. Large knuckle bones are the safest type and even then they should not be cooked, as this hardens them so that they are more likely to damage teeth.

OPPOSITE: *A five-year-old Pyrennean mountain dog exudes good health and contentment.*

Chapter 4
TRAINING
YOUR DOG

Dogs enjoy order and structure in their lives and a well-trained dog is a happy dog.

The dog knows what is expected of it and the owner is relaxed and in control,

which produces an all-round feeling of security and confidence.

Basic dog training is not difficult but it does demand a fair degree of commitment on the part of the owner. Half-hearted training, with the owner giving up whenever patience and persistence is required, is useless and will only leave the dog bewildered and undisciplined. Whether you want a well-mannered pet or a dog capable of winning obedience trials, the earlier you begin, the better.

EARLY LESSONS

Your puppy must learn its name as soon as possible, so decide on a name as soon as you choose your pup and don't chop and change. Use the name every time you speak to the pup, clapping your hands or slapping your leg to catch its attention. When it responds, give plenty of fuss and praise. At the same time, the pup must learn the meaning of the word 'No'. Every

ABOVE: *A Brittany hunting spaniel is schooled to a high level.*

OPPOSITE: *A well-trained dog which sits as its lead is removed.*

time it does something you do not want it to do on a regular basis, look it straight in the eye, wag a stern finger, and give a firm 'No', preferably in a gruff voice resembling a growl. It is much easier to stop problem behaviour arising than to correct it once it has become established.

When you have had the puppy for a week or so, and it has become used to the household routine, take the first step in training with a soft puppy collar. Slip it on your puppy just before its mealtime or before you play a game together, so that the collar is associated with happy times. Take it off after a few minutes, then next time leave it on a little longer, and so on. Within a week, the puppy should be used to the collar and you can then start attaching the leash. Once again put it on just before a meal then carry your puppy to within sight of its bowl. Put it down and hold the leash loosely while the puppy walks forward to eat. Never pull on the leash or the puppy may panic. As it gains confidence, increase the distance between puppy and food, and then try using the leash at times when the puppy would normally be following you around. By the time you are ready to take your puppy outside, it will be fully accustomed to the leash.

TRAINING CLASSES

If you feel you need help in training your puppy, you will probably be able to find a local dog-training class. Most take

OPPOSITE: *Alert and responsive to its owner, an alsatian waits for the signal to 'Come!'.*

BELOW: *Similar looks are virtually all that remain common to the domesticated dog and its wild ancestor, the European wolf.*

ABOVE: *Dogs have no natural sense of what is good or bad behaviour and will do whatever pleases them at the time. It is up to you to show them what behaviour you expect. However, the dog pictured above is a police 'sniffer' dog and although it looks as if it is behaving in an unruly manner, this animal has been trained to a very high degree.*

dogs from six months old and an introductory course, lasting eight or nine weeks will teach basic exercises and give tips on solving problems. However, don't make the mistake of thinking that all you need to do is turn up for class each week. You must practise the techniques you learn and reinforce your puppy's lessons every day or your time will be wasted.

REWARD AND PUNISHMENT

Dogs have no morality, no natural sense of what is 'right' or 'wrong'. They will act in the way that seems most beneficial at the time, so it stands to reason that they are far more likely to

do the things we ask if they expect to gain something by it. In that, they are not too different from humans!

Food rewards can play a crucial role in training. In the wild, much of the dog's waking time would be spent concentrating on finding food and though we provide our pets with enough to eat, this instinct still runs deep and strong. When you plan a training session take a little packet of tidbits along. Whenever the dog hears the bag rustle, it will know that something good is on offer and it can be rewarded with a tidbit when it has obeyed a command. You don't need to worry that a dog will expect a tidbit every time it does as it is told. Once you have practised a command successfully several times, continue to reinforce the behaviour intermittently, giving a tidbit every fourth or sixth time the dog obeys. Soon the dog will respond without the promise of food. All the same, it is best to keep the tidbits very small and not use anything sugary, or your dog will fatten before your eyes. Dry cat-food pellets are a good choice; they are tiny but dogs enjoy them greatly. Take the extra calories into account when planning your dog's diet during the training period.

Teaching a dog to alter its behaviour because it wants to is far more effective than the more punitive methods like jerking painfully at its neck with chains. When your dog has done what is required, be generous with the 'good dog' praise, give your dog a good rub and cuddle or whatever it likes best and it will want to do the same thing again to get the same result. You can often check unwanted behaviour for more successfully by withholding attention than by shouting and threatening. Simply turn away from the dog, and don't look at it or speak to it. A few minutes will be enough; dogs hate to be ignored and they soon get the message.

Misbehaviour can often be nipped in the bud if you act quickly enough. The crucial moment is when the dog is thinking about chasing a cat or jumping up on a forbidden chair. Catch its attention with a sharp 'No!', by clapping your hands or kicking a toy towards the dog. Once you have its attention, give it a pat and a 'good dog'.

BELOW: *It is important to catch misbehaviour and distract the dog before the situation escalates.*

TRAINING TIPS

* ★ Be firm, patient and kind.

* ★ A single member of the family, preferably the 'pack leader', should undertake the early training.

* ★ Keep the sessions short; never persist until the dog is bored.

* ★ Vary the exercises in a training session.

* ★ Avoid battles of will; distract the dog's attention before you reach deadlock.

* ★ Use a long training leash for all early training out of doors.

* ★ Be prepared to repeat the same exercise several times every day.

* ★ Don't move on to the next stage too quickly; make sure that every step has been thoroughly mastered before tackling a new task.

* ★ Decide which word you will use for each command and stick to it, otherwise the dog will become confused.

* ★ Remember that success breeds success. Finish off an unsatisfactory session with a familiar exercise so that the dog can succeed and be praised.

'COME!' TRAINING

This is an exercise you can practise indoors with your puppy. Wait until your dog is looking at you from the other side of the room then, when it begins to move towards you, say 'Come!' and, stooping slightly, extend both arms forwards and slightly sideways in a welcoming gesture. Bend down to the dog's level and give it an enjoyable rub, telling it how well it has done. Use this technique frequently, so that the puppy gets to know the word and the gesture. When you are ready to begin training outside, let the dog trot beside you on the leash, then call its name, say 'Come!' and start walking backwards, giving a gentle pull on the leash, if necessary. The dog will come to look on this as a game and it should respond easily.

OPPOSITE: *Use your dog's natural chasing instinct to teach retrieving. In the early stages of training, your puppy will probably find chewing the ball more fun.*

'COME!' TRAINING

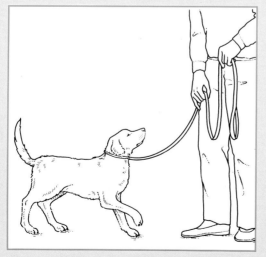

While outside with the dog on the leash, say 'Come!' and walk backwards.

The dog will probably respond in the required manner and when it does, reward it with a pat.

ABOVE: *A water enthusiast enjoys swimming to retrieve sticks.*

LEFT: *Stick retrieval games can become competitive when two dogs are involved.*

'SIT!' TRAINING

This exercise, like 'Come!' makes use of the dog's natural responses. At meal-times, hold the dog's food bowl over its head and say 'Sit!' firmly, with an emphasis on the 't'. If you back the dog so that its rump is near the wall it will probably sit instinctively but if it does not get the idea, put your other hand on its rump and press gently. Insist that it sits properly, rather than a hasty half-squat, wait a couple of seconds, then praise it and put down the food.

ABOVE: *Playtime as well as training is important, particularly for young puppies like these.*

Decide on a release word that can be used whenever an exercise is completed, so that the dog knows it can get up, move off and so on. It might be 'OK', 'Go', 'Off' or anything you like. Your dog will not understand the word itself, only its associations, but don't choose a word that sounds too much like any of the other commands you plan to give.

'SIT AND STAY!'

When the meal-time lesson has been learned, practise outside, holding your hand above the dog's head and giving the same command. The first time, have a tidbit in your hand but after that only give the dog a tidbit now and then. Eventually you can abandon the food rewards altogether.

You can move on to 'Sit and Stay!' when your dog sits when instructed and no longer needs a hand on the rump or the promise of a tidbit – but not before. Have your dog 'Sit!', then raise your hand as a signal. Hold it in front of the dog's face with the palm forward and vertical. Say 'Stay!' and take a step

ABOVE: *A cocker spaniel has mastered the technique of 'Sit and stay!'.*

backwards. Step back towards the dog quite quickly and if it has not moved, praise it or give a tidbit. If it does move, say 'No!' firmly and begin over again.

Once the dog begins to respond to the command 'Stay!', then gradually increase the distance that you move away after giving the command. Keep repeating 'Stay!' and giving the hand signal every few seconds in the early stages. Once the dog has learned to 'stay' on command, raise your hand (holding the training leash) above its head and walk slowly round in a circle. At first the dog will probably turn round with you but each time this happens say 'No!', then begin the exercise again.

'HEEL!'

When training your dog to walk to heel, always keep the dog on the same side. Most trainers keep the dog on the left and carry the leash in the right hand, and you can hold a favourite toy or a bag containing a few tidbits in your left hand. As you step off, say 'Heel!' and give a hand signal, sweeping your left hand forward in front of the dog's nose. Walk your dog briskly and keep its attention by tapping your leg or chatting companionably. Make lots of right turns and occasionally give a tidbit when the dog has its shoulder alongside your left knee. If it

'HEEL!'

It is a good idea to begin any exercise with your dog sitting quietly at your side. As you move off give the 'heel' instruction and sweep your hand forward as a signal (top right). Keep your dog's attention by tapping your leg occasionally (middle left). Give an occasional tidbit while you are working, when the dog has it's nose alongside your left knee. If you pause in the exercise give the 'Sit!' instruction and give a tidbit when the dog obeys (above right). If the dog pulls ahead during exercise (left) give a quick tug on the lead and say 'Heel!'.

LEFT: *Training sessions should not be too long; you will keep the dog's interest alive if you allow plenty of 'free time'.*

BELOW: *The natural guarding instincts of dogs emerge as a visitor approaches the gate.*

pulls forward (most dogs want to walk faster than their owners and to lead the way), give a quick tug on the leash and say 'Heel!' firmly. Don't try to haul your dog backwards or you may end up in a tug of war. If the dog keeps pulling to the left, walk close to a fence or wall. The sessions should not be too long; alternate two or three heeling routines with other exercises to keep the dog's interest.

'FETCH!' TRAINING

Use your dog's natural instinct for chasing a moving object to teach retrieving. Begin with your dog at your left hand side on a long leash and throw a favourite toy a few paces in front of you. Choose something that will bounce or tumble to attract the dog's interest then, as soon as the dog moves to chase the toy, say 'Fetch!'. Once the dog has picked up the toy, let it have fun running about with it for a couple of minutes while you keep the leash slack. Then call 'Come!' and if necessary, pull the leash gently. When the dog returns, have it sit in front of you and offer a tidbit in exchange for the toy. As the dog drops the toy, say 'Give!' or 'Drop!', then give plenty of praise. If the dog drops the toy voluntarily when it returns to you, you should still give the command and the tidbit. As with the other training exercises, phase out the tidbits gradually. Increase the distance you throw the toy little by little then, once the dog is obeying commands well, try the same exercise off the leash – providing of course, that you are in a safe area.

'FETCH!'

As with most exercise, begin with the dog on your left side, holding the long leash in your right hand (top left). A bouncy rubber ball or bone is a good aid for 'Fetch' training (top right). Always give the 'Fetch!' command as you throw it and your dog will soon get the idea. When your dog returns with the ball or bone, have a tidbit ready (left) and the dog should willingly hand over the toy in exchange.

Chapter 5
CARING FOR YOUR DOG

Taking care of your dog means understanding its needs and

natural instincts and being firm as well as being affectionate.

A well-cared for dog is a balanced dog.

Caring successfully for a dog means understanding its instincts and its needs. However humans may have modified dogs in their various breeds, they are all descended from a wild ancestor, the wolf. Though our domestic dogs do not have to hunt for food or protect themselves and their offspring from predators, they retain their hunting and protective instincts, coupled with the keen senses that would have enabled them to survive in the wild.

THE PACK INSTINCT

Dogs are pack animals and every pack has a leader. In the wild, this is the dog who will eat first, select the best and safest sleeping place and be the first to drive off any attack. When you

own a dog, it will regard the members of the household as its pack and normally see its owner as the pack leader. This is the way it should be, but behaviour problems may arise if a dominant dog begins to believe that it is the leader and constantly challenges the owner's authority - pulling on the lead, snatching and 'guarding' toys, growling if you try to move it from your bed. You don't need to behave like an old-time slave-owner to assert your authority but the dog does need to learn its place in the household; useful strategies are outlined in this chapter and in Chapter 6. At the same time, remember that a pack animal needs to socialize and will not be happy if constantly left alone in the house or shut out in the back yard. Your dog needs to be your companion, so if you don't have any time to spend with it, consider buying a goldfish instead.

UNDERSTANDING YOUR DOG

Dogs have the highly developed senses of hunters and scavengers. Their field of vision is much broader than that of humans, because their eyes are set on either side of the head, and though their awareness of colour and detail is probably not as good as ours, they can distinguish the slightest movement from a surprising distance. Unlike cats, they pay little attention to birds and flies because such creatures are out of their reach but anything fast-moving on their level - which may be a car wheel, a bicycle or a pair of running feet, as well as their natural prey - will trigger a chasing response.

The design of their ears and the ability to move each ear independently without necessarily moving the head means that a dog can locate and distinguish sounds with great accuracy over long distances. They will hear the sound of their owner's approach long before any humans in the house are aware of it and can pick out the sound of the family car from all the others on a busy road. They can also hear sounds far too high for the human ear - an ability invaluable in the wild, for many small animals emit ultrasonic sounds and this would enable the dog to locate food.

Smell is the most vital of the senses; the dog's sense of smell being several million times better than that of humans. In the wild they use smell to locate game and in suburbia this can be translated into locating something tempting deep within a dust-bin, often with disastrous results. Smell is also important in social reactions: two dogs meeting will sniff one another thoroughly as an introduction and a dog out walking will want to deposit a little urine on each lamppost and tree, to tell other dogs that it has passed that way. Humans have harnessed the dog's remarkable sense of smell for use in sniffing out drugs or explosives or detecting bodies buried under rubble or in snow-drifts.

BODY LANGUAGE

AN ALERT DOG will have its tail and head up and its ears pricked (according to breed) and if its tail is wagging and its movements are bouncy, it's pretty pleased with life.

A FEARFUL DOG will cringe low with its ears flattened and its tail tucked between its legs.

AN AGGRESSIVE DOG will stand with head and tail held high making itself look as large as possible to create maximum impact. Once the hackles rise along the back and shoulders and the lips curl back to show plenty of teeth, it is thinking about attacking.

A SUBMISSIVE DOG will roll over on its back with its belly exposed and one leg slightly raised.

A PLAYFUL DOG will begin with a 'play-bow', dropping down on its forelimbs with its rump raised in the air, keeping eye contact with the intended playmate. This will usually be followed by a good deal of bouncing around and tail-wagging to encourage the playmate to join in a game. Between two dogs, this usually results in an excited chase and a mock fight.

EXERCISE

Exercise is necessary to a healthy dog, though the amount of exercise differs greatly between breeds. A Chihuahua will be happy with a five-minute stroll twice a day and a West Highland Terrier with a 15-minute walk, but a Labrador Retriever needs an hour's vigorous exercise off the leash and a German Shepherd more like one and a half hours. You can judge whether you are giving your dog enough exercise from its reactions. If it is still bounding about full of energy after your return home after a walk, then the exercise has been insufficient. If it settles down to sleep soon after getting in, you have judged time and distance pretty well.

Dogs need their exercise every single day; a run in the garden on weekdays and long walks at the weekends may suit you, but it will not suit your dog. You can cut down the distance you have to walk by teaching the dog to retrieve, so that it is running back and forth, covering 10 times as much ground as you.

If you are an eager athlete, remember that a young dog will need time to build up its stamina gradually. Too much exercise when the bones and muscles are developing can lead to long-term problems. This applies particularly to the giant breeds as they develop more slowly than smaller dogs and too much exercise under 12 months old can produce muscular and joint disorders later. Older dogs, too, may no longer be able to manage long walks and will be happy with a short stroll or a gentle game in the garden.

OPPOSITE: *Exercise is an important element in a dog's life; it not only enhances its physical wellbeing but also stimulates its senses, keeping it alert and happy.*

Many dogs love to swim and this, too, can be good exercise but choose the location carefully. The water must be reasonably clean, there should be no submerged branches or stakes that could hurt the dog and no strong currents to carry it away. Never let the dog plunge merrily into a river with steep banks so that it will find it difficult to scramble out.

PLAY

Play is essential to your puppy's development and, unlike many other animals, dogs continue to play throughout their lives. Playing games with your dog reinforces the bond between you and gives an outlet for natural canine behaviour that would be seen, in the wild, as it hunted and chased, caught and killed its prey.

A wide range of toys is available in pet shops and you can improvise some very satisfactory playthings without spending money:

BALLS: these should never be smaller than tennis balls for medium-sized dogs and for a larger dogs you should use a bigger size to avoid any possibility of a ball getting lodged in the throat.

SQUEAKY TOYS: they come in all shapes and sizes and dogs love the squeaking, which stimulates them to 'shake and kill'. They should be made of latex as cheaper alternatives can be chewed into pieces and swallowed. Take care with any squeaky toys. Dogs have been known to 'attack' a young child, attracted by a squeaky toy – with tragic consequences.

NYLON CHEWS: these are made from nylon and often shaped like bones. They help keep the teeth and gums healthy but though some dogs seem to enjoy gnawing at them indefinitely, others soon find them boring.

LEFT: *Play fighting with other puppies is often a favourite recreation.*

🐾 **KONGS:** these toys originated in America and are made of chew-resistant rubber which bounces in an unpredictable way. Dogs have a wonderful time with them.

🐾 **FRISBEES:** these are good toys for owner and dog to share but only use those made of light material as they could otherwise cause damage to the dog's mouth and teeth when caught.

🐾 **DUMBBELLS:** these can be made of rubber, wood or canvas and are ideal for retrieving games.

🐾 **TUG TOYS:** dogs always enjoy a tug-of-war, and can play as happily with another dog as with their owner. A knotted rope makes a good alternative. Do not play tugging games with 'mouthy' or very assertive dogs.

🐾 **SUSPENDED ROPE OR CAR TYRE:** some dogs enjoy swinging on anything hanging from a tree and small and medium-sized animals will ride inside a swinging car tyre.

PLAY WARNINGS

Most play sessions are a joy for both owner and dog but dogs do become very excited and it is important to keep things under control. If games are allowed to get out of hand, with the dog feeling that it is stronger than the owner and can always win, it may come to think it is the pack leader and behaviour problems can result.

★ Don't let the dog be the instigator of play sessions; you should decide when they start and finish.

★ Don't let the dog grab and make off with toys which it then refuses to give up. You should be the one to produce the toys and put them away after the game.

★ Don't allow growling, hysterical barking, or jumping up. Stop the game until the dog has calmed down.

★ Don't play wrestling games on the floor, particularly with large dogs.

★ Don't allow the dog to rest its teeth anywhere on your body or clothing, however lightly or playfully.

MEETING A STRANGER

Children brought up with dogs are likely to think that all dogs are as good-tempered and friendly as their own. It is important to teach them a few basic precautions when dealing with dogs.

★ Never try to make friends with a dog that is not accompanied by its owner and always check with the owner before going near the dog or stroking it.

★ Always let the dog see you coming; never approach from behind.

★ If the dog backs away, cringes or lays back its ears, don't touch. This may be more likely to happen if the dog is on a leash, so that it feels trapped.

★ Don't touch the dog's back or hindquarters; stroke its head and neck instead.

★ Never crouch down with your face on a level with the dog's head or try to cuddle it.

TWO-DOG HOUSEHOLDS

There are advantages to owning two dogs, especially if you have to be out a good deal of the time. Boredom problems are far less likely if your dog has a playmate and, when out walking, two dogs can chase around and get far more exercise than you can give on your own.

At the same time, a multi-dog household can bring its problems. If you already own a pushy, assertive dog, it is wise to choose a submissive dog as its companion. Though two bitches, or a dog and a bitch, will usually get on well enough, two dominant dogs in the same household may war constantly for top position. Your instinct will be to bring your dogs up as equals, but this is asking for trouble. Dogs will sort out their own hierarchy and you should recognize this and treat them accordingly. Some owners are puzzled that their dogs seem to get along perfectly well when they are not with them - playing in the garden, curling up together in bed - but start scrapping once the

ABOVE: *Labradors are justifiably popular family pets because of their gentle temperament.*

GARDEN SAFETY

No dog should ever be allowed in the street without supervision but there will be times you will want to put your dog out in the garden for a while to get rid of excess energy or simply sit in the sun. First of all, make sure the garden is as safe as you can make it.

FENCES: They should be high enough to prevent a dog jumping over and they must be kept in good repair, as a dog will find any hole or loose board.

GATES: Cover them with wire mesh if your dog is small enough to squeeze through and cover the gap at the bottom with a wire mesh strip to discourage burrowing and digging.

FISH PONDS: Cover securely with wire mesh.

WOODWORK: Some wood preservatives can be toxic to chewing dogs so check that anything you use is safe.

SLUG-BAIT: Metaldehyde, often used to kill slugs, is poisonous to dogs but less harmful preparations are available.

HERBICIDE: Many herbicdes contain substances harmful to animals. Be guided by the label.

ANTIFREEZE: Ethylene glycol, contained in anti-freeze, has a sweet taste that is very attractive to dogs but is highly toxic, so wipe up any spills carefully and keep cans locked way.

PLANTS: Some plants, like laburnum, mistletoe berries, lupins and yew are harmful to dogs so don't keep them in a garden where a dog is loose. Keep your daffodil bulbs out of the way, too.

owner comes on the scene. This is because they are refusing to recognize the dominant dog's status and are trying to 'even things up' all the time, so that the dog has to assert itself constantly. If you greet the dominant dog first, put down its food bowl first and so on, both dogs will accept this quite happily and there will be no need for fights.

DOGS AND CHILDREN

Helping to care for a dog can be a valuable learning experience, as well as a source of pleasure, for children. It can teach them a sense of responsibility and develop their protective instincts. However, even if a dog 'belongs' to a child, no youngster under 10 should be given sole care of a pet; instead they should be involved with feeding, grooming and walking the dog, always under adult supervision. Children of 11 and over should be capable of taking a dog for a short walk alone but only if the dog is of a suitable size. It is unfair and unwise to expect a child to control a large, powerful dog which might be tempted to chase a cat or fight an aggressor. Some dog training clubs have classes for young handlers.

Never let yourself become careless about contact between children and dogs. Dogs may mistake the signals that humans give out and react in a way that is perfectly natural for them but

GROOMING EQUIPMENT

- 🐾 Body brush

- 🐾 Bristle brush

- 🐾 Wide-toothed comb

- 🐾 Fine-toothed comb (for breeds with fine coats)

- 🐾 Grooming mitten (hound glove)

- 🐾 Carder

- 🐾 Blunt-nosed scissors

- 🐾 Chamois leather

- 🐾 Cotton wool/cotton wool buds

comes as an ugly shock to us. When your child has friends round, their play can be very boisterous and the dog may mistake the excited, jerky movements of children for aggression and think that it needs to defend a member of the family. If a visiting child is nipped, scolding the dog will be useless, as it will have no idea what it has done wrong. Proper control and supervision will prevent any such misunderstandings.

GROOMING YOUR DOG

Long-haired dogs will need daily grooming; it is unwise to skip the chore for several days only to find that you have to deal with matted lumps, which will hurt the dog and cause it to

BELOW: *Long-haired dogs, such as this blue Afghan, require daily grooming.*

The technique for grooming a long-haired dog is the most time-consuming:

STEP 1 Begin with the hind legs. Lift the outer hair and brush the undercoat thoroughly. Then brush the topcoat down smoothly and follow by combing from root to tip. Repeat with the front legs.

STEP 2 Hold up the dog's head, brush down the throat and between the forelegs. Brush the fine hair of the stomach with firm but gentle strokes, right from the roots, paying special attention to any bits of twig or grass seeds that might be caught in the coat.

STEP 3 Brush, then comb, the body from shoulders to rump, dealing with the undercoat first, then the topcoat.

STEP 4 Comb the long hair of the ears and around the face, but you should be very gentle in this area. Comb out the feathering of the tail and on the back of the legs in some breeds.

STEP 5 Wipe each eye with a damp ball of cotton wool to clean away tear-staining or loose hair. Use a fresh pad of damp cotton wool to clean around the nose. You can clean out the folds of the ears with damp

cotton buds but *never* poke them into the ears themselves.

STEP 6 Check the paws carefully; remove any grit or grass seeds from between the toes and trim away excess fur with blunt-nosed scissors.

STEP 7 Give the coat a final polish with a chamois leather kept specially for the purpose.

If your dog has a light-coloured coat, it may benefit from dry shampooing. This is no sub-stitute for a bath but it can remove grease and make the coat look cleaner, thus avoiding excessive washing, which can be detrimental to the coat. The powder is sprinkled on, left a short time, then brushed out thoroughly.

resist grooming in the future. Short-haired breeds will need less attention but regular grooming is important for every type of dog. It massages the skin, stimulates the circulation and improves your pet's general condition; it removes tangles and any foreign bodies stuck in the hair; and it removes dead hair which will otherwise be shed all over your furniture.

During grooming your dog should be at a height comfortable for you: small dogs can be groomed on your lap but for larger breeds it will be more convenient to stand the dog on an old table. Each breed has its own requirements and the equipment you will need may vary. A smooth-haired dog can be groomed with a body brush while others will need a bristle brush to do the job satisfactorily. A carder (rectangular board with wire teeth) is ideal for dealing with the undercoat of short-haired dogs, while a rubber grooming mitten will remove dead hair from the outer coat.

GROOMING A SHORT-HAIRED DOG

This is a much quicker and simpler job but should not be neglected. Dogs kept indoors will moult all year round, so regularly grooming is in your own interest. Use a bristle brush to remove dead hair and skin, working up from the rump to the head in sections, making sure that the whole coat is groomed. If the dog has any feathering on its tail, use a comb to run through it. Finally, finish off the coat with a chamois leather to give a good shine.

PROFESSIONAL GROOMING

Some dogs, like Poodles, do not shed hair. Instead it keeps on growing so they need clipping every six to eight months – hence the popularity of 'poodle parlours'. Spaniels may also need clipping, English Sheepdogs often have their coats cut short in the summer and Wire-haired Terriers need stripping twice a year. Though these tasks can all be undertaken by a knowledgeable owner, many people prefer to put their dogs in the hands of an expert.

BATHING YOUR DOG

Dogs should not be bathed more often than absolutely necessary as it removes natural oils from the coat and may leave it looking dull. However, some owners are more sensitive to 'doggy' smells than others and some dogs love to roll in anything unpleasant. Also, dogs needing regular clipping or stripping are usually bathed beforehand, so that the hair is easier to handle.

Follow a simple bathing routine:

STEP 1 You will need canine shampoo, a jug for pouring water, several towels and, for a small dog, a plastic bowl or an old baby-bath. A larger dog may have to stand in the family bath tub or, in fine weather, on a concrete patio near a drain outlet. Wear a plastic apron or put on a raincoat back to front.

STEP 2 Plug the dog's ears with cotton wool and stand it in the bath in 6cm (2in) of warm water. A rubber mat on the bottom of the bath will help stop it slipping about.

STEP 3 Pour warm water over the dog's coat, starting at the hindquarters and working forwards. Use the shampoo to work up a lather, massaging against the lie of the coat. Make sure the underside and the legs are washed thoroughly.

STEP 4 With a little shampoo on your fingertips, lather the head gently. Be careful to keep shampoo away from the eyes and mouth.

STEP 5 Rinse and dry the head.

STEP 6 Rinse the rest of the body with warm water and be sure that every vestige of soap is removed.

STEP 7 Squeeze as much excess water as possible from the coat and legs. Lift the dog out of the bath and wrap it in a towel, rubbing vigorously.

STEP 8 If your dog will allow it, use a hairdrier on a low setting. Long coats should be groomed into place while drying, just like a 'blow-dry' at the hairdresser. Otherwise use a second towel and a third if necessary.

Chapter 6
SOLVING BEHAVIOUR PROBLEMS

Every time your dog settles down in your best armchair or launches itself in delight

at a visiting neighbour, it is establishing a habit and the longer the habit is allowed to persist,

the more time and effort it will take you to put things right.

It may be amusing when your excited puppy strains at the leash or begs a biscuit from your plate but it is not nearly so funny when your full-grown dog drags you round the park or steals your guest's sandwich from under his nose.

Bad behaviour needs to be tackled with firmness and consistency. Correct, rather than punish, the dog. Punishment is pointless unless administered at the moment of misbehaviour; just a few seconds later, the dog has no idea why you are being unkind.

JUMPING UP

You may not mind your joyful dog leaping to greet you but your visitors certainly will; such behaviour can terrify young children and is dangerous to the elderly, who may be knocked off their feet.

OPPOSITE: *Begging tricks are amusing when kept under control, but the dog will find it hard to understand why 'trick begging' is acceptable but pestering for food whenever it feels inclined is not.*

If the dog is large, an effective method can be bringing up your knee into the dog's chest each time it tries to jump up. If that sounds over athletic, try catching hold off the dog's paws, one in each hand. Don't speak to your dog but look over its head and hold out its paws, without squeezing, until it is struggling to get away. When all four paws are firmly on the floor bend down to the dog's level to greet and pet it.

You will need to make sure that every member of the household uses the same procedure and uses it every single time - it is no use expecting a dog to understand the difference between welcome dry paws and unwelcome muddy ones. When visitors come, put on the dog's collar and leash, give the command 'sit', then wait until the dog is obedient and quiet before allowing it free for a greeting.

BARKING

Protecting the home is a dog's natural instinct and most owners welcome barking that warns off intruders but 20 minutes of barking every time the doorbell rings can become very trying indeed.

ABOVE: *Some dogs develop a habit of becoming over-excited every time a walk is in prospect.*

For re-training, you will need the help of a friend who will walk briskly up to the door then, once the barking is under way, retreat quietly. Allow the dog half a dozen barks, then distract its attention: some trainers bang a metal tray on a table, crash two baking tins together or use a rape alarm, others find

that a water-pistol will do the trick with far less noise. When it stops barking, give a tidbit and plenty of praise. Once peace has descended, your helper can move off again and the process is repeated. Once the dog gets the general idea, lengthen the time between the end of barking and giving the tidbit, so that the dog has to remain quiet for several seconds before getting the reward. With patience, you should be able to train your dog to stop lengthy barking sessions without discouraging it from giving a necessary warning.

Some dogs become hysterical with excitement every time a walk is in prospect, with a tirade of high-pitched barking which fills the street as you set off and only subsides when the walk is well under way.

If this habit is causing you problems, set aside some time to work on it. Next 'walkies' time, put on the dog's collar, then put on your coat, pick up the leash and walk towards the door as usual. When the barking starts, say 'No!' in your most formidable voice. Then take off your coat, put down the leash and sit down with the newspaper. Once the dog has been quiet for a few minutes, go through the whole routine again and be prepared to repeat it a dozen times if necessary. Only take the walk when your dog can approach the door without barking.

DOGS ON FURNITURE

Some dogs take it as their right to occupy the best armchair or spread themselves across the bed. No matter how many times you order them off, they will take up their favourite position the moment your back is turned. The problem usually starts in the early days, when the owner cuddles a puppy on his or her lap all evening or makes a habit of taking it to bed. It is not surprising if, not that long afterwards, a large animal is monopolizing the furniture.

You can try discouraging a dog from using your bed by putting a sheet of aluminium foil under the blanket but better still, keep the bedroom door shut. Deny access to the easy chairs by upending a dining chair or a cardboard box on them until your dog gets the idea.

COPROPHAGIA

Eating faeces is not such a revolting habit as it appears; in the wild dogs obtain useful nutrients from their own faeces and those of other animals. The habit is often seen in young dogs, whose bodies need a high level of nutrients, but it usually stops spontaneously. If it carries on into adulthood, the first thing you should do is check with your veterinarian: the dog may have worms, or some gastric upset may be preventing the proper absorption of nutrients.

If there is no health problem, make sure that your dog feels full and satisfied by adding root vegetables or bran to its meals or feeding a dry, high-fibre diet. It may help to increase the food allowance or to spread it over three or four meals during the day. In addition, you might try adding some canned pineapple to the dog's meals: there's something about the smell or taste this gives to the faeces that makes them far less attractive as a food supplement.

BELOW: *Unless it is firmly discouraged, a dog soon feels it has every right to occupy the best place on the sofa.*

DESTRUCTIVENESS

Some dogs chew slippers, books and the children's toys, others gnaw at furniture and carpets. The real hard cases rip the paper from the walls and decorate the floorboards with teeth marks. When puppies are teething they will chew anything. This is normal, unstoppable behaviour and you should take all steps to minimize the damage by keeping the house extra tidy and shutting away all tempting objects. Think of the puppy as an energetic toddler who will grab at anything within reach.

If a dog continues chewing, becoming more destructive as its jaws become more powerful, the underlying problem may be boredom. Try giving extra exercise and training sessions as well as plenty of retrieving games to work off your dog's energy. If you are out for a good part of the day, leaving your dog alone, feed in the morning so that it will spend some of the time sleeping. If you leave behind a large marrowbone, a cardboard box and a piece of wood (non-splintering), the dog may gnaw on these in preference to your table legs. There is no harm in giving an old slipper for chewing - so long as the new ones are stowed away. Keep a box for the dog's toys - old socks, rubber rings, balls, pieces of blanket - so that it can forage for something new to worry. When you are in the house, keep an eye on the dog and whenever its eye strays to a forbidden object, distract it with a sharp 'No!' coupled with the dog's name. Once you have its attention, call it over, pet and praise it.

If, while you are retraining your dog, your home is still being demolished, you may have to confine it to one room where it can do minimal damage or to an indoor or outdoor kennel, when unsupervised.

BELOW: *Irish setter puppies chewing a glove. Make sure the puppy has its own toys to chew so that it leaves the family's alone.*

DO'S AND DONT'S FOR IMPROVING BEHAVIOUR

DO look at the problem from the dog's point of view: this could well explain why it is happening.

DON'T hit a 'bad' dog under any circumstances and don't lose your temper; use your tone of voice to indicate displeasure.

DO remember that prevention is better than cure; avoid situations which prompt problem behaviour.

DON'T leave your dog to its own devices for so long that it becomes bored.

DO give plenty of praise when your dog responds to correction or switches attention from unwanted behaviour.

ABOVE: *An indoor kennel promotes a feeling of security and often solves separation anxiety problems in dogs.*

SOILING

Often dogs that are perfectly continent when their owners are present will urinate or defecate when left alone overnight, or when you go out in the daytime. This is brought on by the stress and anxiety of separation and any shouting or punishment will only add to that anxiety and make things worse.

If the problem only occurs at night, the answer may be to put your dog to bed in an indoor kennel. It may look like a prison to you, but it has the effect of making the dog feel more secure and it is most unlikely to foul its own bed. Of course, if you do this, it is essential that the dog is taken out to relieve itself last thing at night. When it performs in the right place, give plenty of praise and perhaps a tidbit.

Dogs suffering from separation anxiety when their owners go shopping or have a night out at the theatre tend to be those that seldom let their owners out of their sight, even sharing their beds at night. They need to be helped to adjust gradually to separation and, once again, the indoor kennel may be the answer. Begin by putting the dog in the kennel for five minutes a day. Stay in the same room, but ignore the dog while it is in the kennel, however much it protests. Increase the time until the dog is spending an hour in the kennel but don't leave it alone until it is completely relaxed and happy about the kennel. By the time you can go out of the room without causing distress, the dog will probably look on the kennel as a secure den and you can start leaving the kennel door open so that it can come and go as it pleases. You will probably find that when you go out, the dog will bed down in its kennel until you return and the level of stress will have reduced considerably.

FEARS OF LOUD NOISES

Many dogs are scared by sudden loud noises and crouch quivering under the table every time an aircraft passes overhead or wrap themselves in the curtain when they hear a gun go off.

MAKING FRIENDS

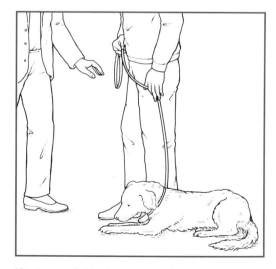

If it is unreliable, bring your dog in on a leash to greet a new visitor.

Once the dog is calm, the visitor can approach quietly.

LEFT: *Border collie puppies play tug-of-war with a soft toy.*

the household *(see Chapter 5)*. If the dog finds that growling or snapping means that it gets its own way, it will growl and snap more frequently. If it finds that any such behaviour results in a period of being ignored or sent to its bed, the dog will soon see that menacing humans is a bad idea. Take no chances with a dog that shows aggressive tendencies; use a muzzle when grooming, bathing or dressing a wound and if your own efforts at solving the problem get nowhere, seek professional help.

This can become a problem if you live on a flightpath or on the edge of a country estate renowned for its shooting. Many owners unintentionally make things worse by fussing over a frightened dog, which has the effect of giving a reward and so reinforcing its behaviour.

Never give a dog any of your own tranquillizers; if you think tranquillizers are necessary, ask your veterinarian to prescribe something suitable. Overcoming fear means desensitizing the dog and this means time and trouble. You will need to tape-record the frightening noise, then begin by playing it quietly in the background while you are playing with the dog or feeding it. Increase the volume gradually and be prepared to turn it down and proceed more slowly if the dog shows signs of fear. Once you can play the sound loudly without reaction from the dog, it is time to take the dog outside and expose it to the actual noise, still distracting it with play and treats, so that it comes to associate the noise with pleasant things.

It may be possible to desensitize your dog to thunderstorms in a similar manner but atmospheric changes, not to mention lightning, accompany the noise of a thunderclap and may be just as unsettling for your dog. In any case, thunderstorms are not so frequent that your dog's reaction is likely to cause much inconvenience. It may be easier to provide a cosy bed in a cupboard or under the stairs, where your dog can hide out until the storm is over.

AGGRESSION

This is the most serious canine behaviour problem as, if it gets out of hand, aggression can lead to actual bodily harm to family members or even strangers and could even mean a death sentence for your dog. Take action to stem any aggressive tendencies as soon as they show themselves; a puppy should never get away with growling when a toy is taken away or when a visitor walks into the house. Never let your dog get the upper hand in

ABOVE: *Calm, confident English setters have been trained not to flinch at sudden noises.*

AGGRESSION TOWARDS VISITORS

A dog that treats welcome visitors like burglars, barking incessantly or baring its teeth in a growl as they step inside, is not an asset to any home and the dog's attitude will not improve if you take the easy way out and shut it away in the kitchen until your visitors have left.

Ask friends who are used to dogs to help you alter the way your dog views visitors in the home. Don't let the dog rush into the hall, barking frantically at the sound of the doorbell, and do not engage in a tug-of-war as the dog lunges for the visitor. Shut the dog in the kitchen, then bring it out on a leash, once the visitor is sitting down. Many visitor confrontations happen because the dog feels threatened by a stranger who stares down from a great height, then bends down over the dog's head, hand outstretched. It is best if your sitting visitor does not look in the dog's direction to begin with and ignores it completely. At any sign of aggression from the dog, give a sudden jerk on the leash - *not* to haul the dog towards you, but to win its attention.

Once the dog has got used to the idea of a stranger in its home, the visitor can produce a tidbit and, still without looking at the dog, hold it alongside his knee, on the flat of the palm. Let the dog come to investigate in its own time but keep hold of the leash and be ready to act if necessary. Once the dog has accepted the tidbit, the visitor should wait for further friendly overtures before speaking to the dog or attempting to pet it. Do make sure that your helper is at ease with dogs and will make no sudden nervous movements.

OPPOSITE: *Many dogs become especially jealous and protective of their bones. You can train your dog to 'share' its bones.*

BELOW: *Aggressive dogs, which 'welcome' visitors with bared teeth and frantic barking, can be cured of their anti-social behaviour.*

AGGRESSION TOWARDS OTHER DOGS

When you are walking out of doors, in an area where you meet and pass other dogs, your normally peaceful dog may become over-protective, or jealous about other dogs coming near you, so that it attempts to drive other animals away. Owners sometimes make matters worse by taking a stick to ward off other dogs - which can only increase aggression from both animals - or hauling their pet off like an unwilling prisoner every time another dog comes in sight.

A dog prone to chasing and fighting should always be on a leash outside its own garden and when you pass another dog, make sure that your body is *between* the two animals. If your dog shows too much interest in a potential adversary, use its name, jerk the leash, then turn round sharply, so that your dog finds itself quickly walking away from its enemy. Keep talking to your dog and praise it for doing well.

Never intervene in a dog fight: you will probably get bitten, either by your own dog or another. If your dog has a propensity for fighting, take a rape alarm along with you; the shock may bring the fight to a stop. If you are near enough to home, a bucket of water thrown over the dogs can do the trick.

ABOVE: *Feral dogs scavenging for scraps of food should not be approached as they are likely to be aggressive.*

AGGRESSION TOWARDS FAMILY MEMBERS

Some dogs resent sharing their pack leader and give all their devotion to one family member, seeing the rest as rivals and warning them off. In this case, the chosen person should no longer be responsible for feeding or walking the dog, but these tasks should be shared around the family - or if the dog shows resentment or jealousy towards one particular family member, that person should become the food and 'walkies' provider.

GUARDING FOOD

This is another form of aggression, when the dog will hunch growling over its food when anyone comes near, or perhaps snap at any hand that strays too close. Any such tendencies in puppies can be prevented at the outset by handfeeding a puppy with food from its bowl and by frequently adding something to the bowl while the puppy is eating, so that it becomes accustomed to approaching hands bringing treats. Many dogs become especially jealous over bones, so when you give your dog a bone, make sure that it gets used to giving it back. Offer a delicious tidbit then, as the dog shows interest, say 'good dog' and exchange the bone for the tidbit. When the dog has finished the treat, return the bone. It will soon get used to the idea that giving up a bone is in its own interest.

If an adult dog is showing this type of aggression, try feeding it in a different place - perhaps a different room, the garage or garden, and feed on a plate rather than in a bowl. Many dogs seem to associate guarding with a bowl or a particular place and this may do the trick. If not, put the plate on a box so that it is level with the dog's shoulder and it can no longer hunch over it. Then try exchanging the plate for a tidbit, as described above.

BELOW: *Walking to heel is a good discipline to encourage and makes for a relaxing walk.*

PULLING ON LEAD

If you dog habitually drags you along the road, even wrapping you round lampposts and trees, good obedience training and plenty of practice in 'heeling' (see Chapter 4) is the best answer. However, you may find that using a head halter on your dog will bring about a dramatic improvement, as you will be able to 'steer' the dog without pulling, jerking and straining. Make sure that the head halter is not too tight and that the dog can pant freely when wearing it. Fit the head halter for the first time during a play session and carry on playing, giving an occasional tidbit so that your dog has little time to fuss about it. Later in the session attach the leash but leave it slack and don't attempt to lead the dog until it has recovered from any initial worries.

STEALING FOOD

Raiding the table, kitchen work surfaces or even the refrigerator for food is a habit that grows very easily in dogs fed scraps at family meal-times, biscuits at elevenses and tasty morsels of meat as you prepare the dinner. Dogs have no morals about stealing and for ever afterwards, anything tasty that comes within reach will be gobbled up.

Obviously the best remedy is to keep all unattended food out of the dog's reach (this includes the rubbish, if your dog is in the habit of raiding) and to fit secure catches on any vulnerable cupboard doors. This may be harder with the refrigerator, and many a resourceful dog has learned that a feast of goodies lie behind the white door, but a small kitchen stepladder, folded and balanced against the door should stop that particular trick. Even if the dog is persistent enough to get the door open in spite of the stepladder, it will then overbalance and send the dog off.

Aversion therapy can be useful in deterring a dog from stealing morsels from the table or kitchen worktops. Fill a chocolate, a sausage roll or anything that will prove irresistible to the dog with mustard or hot pepper sauce and leave it on the table when you leave the room, after instructing the dog with 'Leave' and 'No' and any other forbidding words you normally use. If, when you return, you find that the dog has obeyed, give lots of fuss and praise. Repeat the exercise until the dog has either learned to 'leave' when told or has learned that stolen food tastes very unpleasant.

Chapter 7
YOUR DOG ON
THE MOVE

Most dogs will be much happier being with you on trips or on local car journeys than

staying at home alone, providing their introduction to travel is happy and their first experiences

are not associated with travel sickness or a frightening visit to the veterinarian.

CAR TRAVEL

Accustom your puppy to car travel as soon as possible, with short trips round the block before taking it on a long journey. If it shows any signs of nervousness, play a game in the stationary car or feed your dog in the back. Sometimes rescued dogs, with a bad experience in their past, are terrified of the car, but they can be re-trained, given time and patience. Leave all the car doors open as it stands in your drive and play a chase game which involves the dog scrambling through the car and out the other side. You can then progress to a game which involves you sitting in the car and the dog jumping in and out to claim a toy from you, or perhaps play a tug-of-war. Once the dog is accus-

tomed to the car as a non-fearsome part of its life, try shutting the door, then start the engine without going anywhere. Keep the first trips very short and stop for a walk or a run, so that the dog begins to think of them as a treat. Once the dog is able to travel without distress, you can lengthen the journey, without stopping for a run.

SAFETY IN THE CAR

Dogs should never be completely free in the car; it is not safe for you or for them. An excited dog may jump about and interfere with your concentration and even a perfectly behaved dog can easily be thrown through the air if you have to make an emergency stop. If you have a minor accident, it may escape onto the road in the general confusion and run under the wheels of another car.

You can have a safety belt fitted for your dog, just as for your human passengers, but the dog will probably be more comfortable behind a dog grille, as it will have more freedom of movement. A lightweight adjustable grille will be sufficient for small dogs but larger breeds will require a grille that is fixed to the

OPPOSITE: *Once accustomed to car travel, many dogs actively enjoy spending time in a vehicle.*

TRAVEL TIPS

★ Take your dog for a run beforehand; this gives it an opportunity to get rid of excess energy as well as passing urine and faeces.

★ Never leave your dog in a hot car for more than a few minutes, even with the window open. The car will heat up like a greenhouse and your dog can die of heatstroke remarkably quickly.

★ Take a bottle of water and your dog's waterbowl and give drinks at frequent intervals in warm weather.

★ Have a supply of kitchen paper handy in case of sickness.

★ Don't let your dog stick its head out of an open window. A foreign body may damage its eye.

★ Stop every two or three hours so that the dog can stretch its legs and do what is necessary but always keep it on the leash.

structure of the car. An alternative is a dog-cage that can be assembled in the back of the car or, for small dogs, the type of carriers used for transporting cats.

Plastic-coated wire carriers are airy, long-lasting and easy to clean, but a dog prone to car sickness may be better off if it cannot see the countryside rolling by. In this case, a fibre-glass case with plenty of air vents at the side and a plastic-coated wire door, so that the dog can see you and its surroundings in the car, may be a good choice. Wicker carriers are also available but they are difficult to clean properly.

TRAVEL SICKNESS

Many dogs suffer from travel sickness and most experts advise not feeding the dog for at least three or four hours before a journey, to cut down the likelihood of illness, but some dogs fare better with a small meal shortly before setting out, to settle their stomachs. Unfortunately, there is only one way of finding out which is better for your dog! Adequate ventilation in the car will help and you could try giving your dog a rounded teaspoon of glucose powder dissolved in two tablespoons of water just before the journey.

If, in spite of all precautions, your dog is still sick, your veterinarian may be able to prescribe a sedative for long journeys, though this may be inadvisable for midsummer travel, as sedatives can interfere with the heat regulation of your dog's body.

MOVING HOUSE

Few dogs are bothered by moving house; so long as they are with their pack, a change of surroundings worries them very little. However, the move itself, involving strangers constantly taking things from the dog's territory, is liable to stimulate a good deal of barking and over-excitement. For the sake of peace, it may be wise to ask a friend or relative to take the dog for the day, then take it to the new house when everything is relatively settled.

A young or newly rescued dog may become confused over toilet arrangements in new surroundings and if you find this happening, go back to the puppy toilet-training routine: take the dog to the appropriate area of the garden first thing in the morning, last thing at night and after meals and wait there with it for a few minutes. You should not have to repeat this for more than a couple of days.

RIGHT: *Allow plenty of ventilation if you leave your dog in the car for any length of time, but do not allow your dog to lean out of the window when the care is under way.*

HOLIDAY DOG

Your dog will enjoy a holiday just as much as the rest of the family and there should be no major problem, so long as you plan well.

🐾 Book well ahead and make sure that every hotel or motel on your itinerary accepts dogs. The same applies to rented holiday homes and campsites.

🐾 Check whether an extra charge is made for pets.

🐾 Ask, when booking, if there is a suitable area nearby where you can walk the dog.

🐾 Take your dog's bed, toys, food bowls and enough food for the first 24 hours at least. Remember that buying at small shops in the country can be expensive.

🐾 Check on the policy regarding dogs at your chosen resort; some forbid dogs on beaches.

🐾 Equip your dog (even a good swimmer) with a lifejacket if you take it out in a boat, just as you do your children.

🐾 Do not allow your dog to drink seawater. If it should do so, give plenty of fresh water afterwards

🐾 Keep your dog quiet and under control at all times, and do not leave it unattended for long periods.

BOARDING KENNELS

If you cannot take your dog with you on holiday, it is not a good idea to leave it in the house, with a friend or 'sitter' coming a couple of times a day to feed and exercise it. Dogs can become very miserable without companionship and you may find that behaviour problems follow. If you can't persuade a friend or relative to take the dog into their home, at least during the daytime, for the duration of the holiday, it is probably in the dog's interest to find a good boarding kennels.

The best way to find a good boarding establishment is through the recommendation of satisfied customers, so ask around among dog owners. Local veterinarians will be able to suggest kennels with a good standard of care. Always inspect the them yourself and ask the owners plenty of questions. Some kennels may not allow you to take the dog's bedding or toys, and you may feel that this indicates an unsympathetic attitude towards their boarders and prefer to take your business elsewhere. Any good kennels will insist on proof of up-to-date vaccinations for distemper, leptospirosis, infectious hepatitis and parvovirus and some also require vaccination against kennel cough.

When you visit the kennels, check the following:

★ The accommodation should be clean, without any strong odours.

★ Each dog should have a snug, peaceful place to sleep and an outdoor run. Concrete is the most hygienic for runs; grass is impossible to disinfect.

★ Built-in heating should be available in cold weather; there should be no free-standing units.

★ The accommodation should have a double door system, so that if a dog escapes from one section, it cannot get out of the unit.

★ Beds must be easy to disinfect.

★ Food should not be left down long after mealtimes and every dog should have fresh water available at all times.

★ Dogs should be walked at least twice a day; check exactly how much exercise your dog will get.

★ Grooming should be available for long-haired dogs; check how often and how thoroughly your dog will be groomed.

If your dog needs any extra care, check whether this can be provided. Some kennels will not accept bitches likely to come into heat, as this creates a furore among the other dogs, so check your calendar and if this is likely to be a problem, consult your veterinarian about the possibility of stopping a heat. Advise the kennel owners of any past medical problems and leave your usual veterinarian's number.

BELOW: *A good kennels should provide each dog with a warm place to sleep and an outdoor run.*

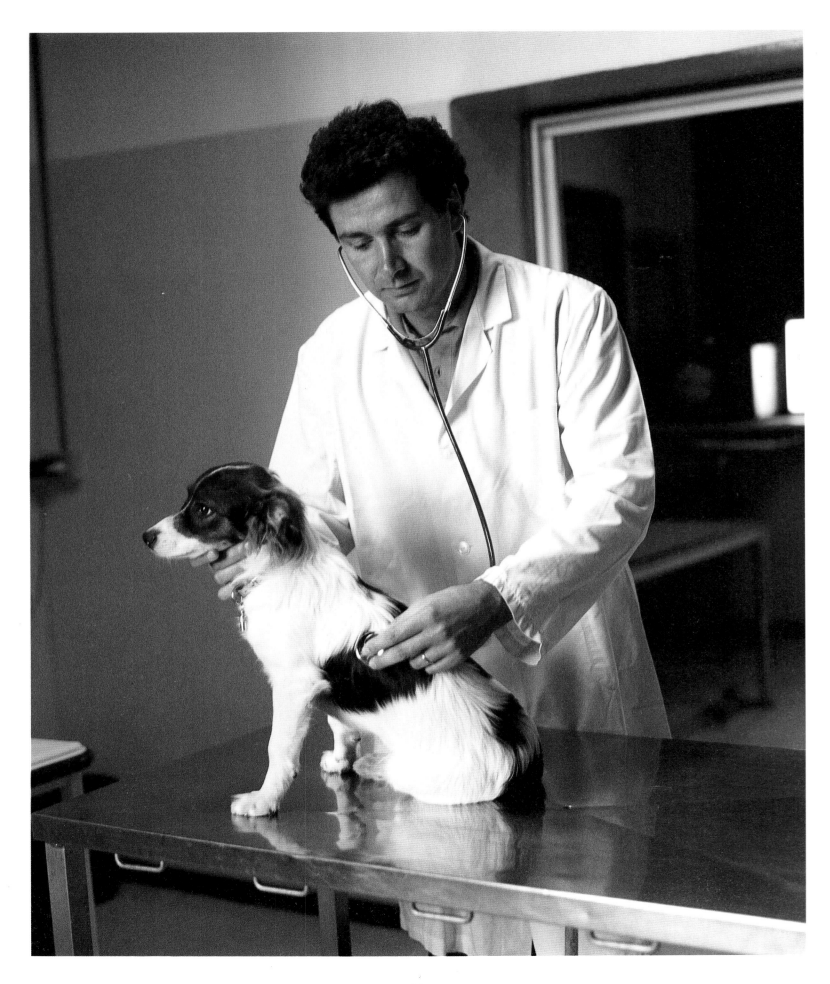

Chapter 8
HEALTH CARE

Your dog cannot talk and tell you when it is ill or in pain,

so your best guide to your pet's health is

your own observation.

Dogs are creatures of habit and, though the odd 'not-too-well' day may mean nothing, if they act in an uncharacteristic manner for longer than that, they may need a veterinary checkup. Using the dog's nose as the barometer of health is very unwise - many a healthy dog may have a dry nose, while the nose of a sickly animal may remain wet. A more reliable guide is your dog's general behaviour: if it is listless, irritable and indifferent when you suggest a game or a walk, there may be a problem. If your dog shows any of the following symptoms, you should take it to the veterinarian immediately (if you go away on holiday ensure that your carer has this list):

* Excessive thirst
* Eating little or nothing for more than 24 hours
* Straining to pass urine
* Generally dull or lethargic appearance
* Noticeable weight loss (You can check the dog's weight by weighing yourself, then picking up the dog and comparing the two weights)
* Bleeding from the mouth, nose, anus or genitals
* Lameness, difficulty in movement or over-sensitivity when touched

The charts overleaf give general guidelines on whether or not veterinary attention is necessary immediately when your dog displays certain symptoms but if you are in any doubt about your dog's condition, don't hesitate: ring the veterinary surgery right away. If you outline the symptoms clearly, the staff will be able to tell you whether an early appointment is necessary.

OPPOSITE: *If you are in any doubt about your dog's condition, take it to the veterinarian immediately.*

VOMITING

WHAT TO CHECK

Has the dog been over-eating?
Has the dog been over-excited?
Has the dog been eating grass?

Has the vomiting continued for
24 hours or is it very frequent?

Is there blood in the vomit?

Does the dog have other signs of
illness (eg diarrhoea, lethargy,
dull looks)?

WHAT TO DO

If no other worrying signs, give no
food overnight, then feed a
light meal.

Consult your veterinarian without
delay.

Digestive disorders can be serious.

DIARRHOEA

WHAT TO CHECK

Has the dog's diet been changed
recently?
Could the dog have been scavenging
in rubbish bins?
Has the dog been drinking milk?

Has the diarrhoea continued for
more than 24 hours?
Is there blood in the faeces?
Does the dog have any signs of
illness (eg vomiting, lethargy,
dull looks?)

WHAT TO DO

If the dog seems well otherwise, give
no food overnight then feed a
bland meal.
If the problem does not recur,
there is no need to worry.

Consult your veterinarian without
delay.
Digestive disorders can be
serious.

COUGHING

WHAT TO CHECK

Has the dog just come in from
the garden?
Have you just sprayed the house with
air freshener etc?

Is the cough harsh and nagging,
sometimes ending in frothing?
Does the dog's breathing seem
abnormal?
Is the dog coughing at night or
on waking?

Does the dog have any other
symptoms (eg lack of appetite, nasal
discharge, lethargy)?

WHAT TO DO

The dog may simply be reacting to
irritation in the respiratory system
from fumes, pollen or insecticide,
grass seeds. Listen for more
persistent coughing.

Consult the veterinarian without
delay.
Your dog may be suffering from
kennel cough or a lung problem.

URINARY PROBLEMS

WHAT TO CHECK

Is your dog straining to pass urine?
Is there blood in the urine?

Is the dog constantly licking its
genital area?

Is the dog urinating more
frequently and drinking a lot?
Is its appetite poor?
Does it have bad breath?

WHAT TO DO

Consult your veterinarian
immediately.

This may be an infection or
stones in the bladder or urethra.

Consult your veterinarian
immediately in case of a kidney
problem.

SCRATCHING

WHAT TO CHECK

Are there black specks visible
in the dog's coat?

Are there any grey insects or white
'nits' visible?

Are there any bald patches or sores?

Are there any pea-sized swellings
on the skin?

WHAT TO DO

Use flea powder or spray; follow
manufacturer's instructions.

Your veterinarian will prescribe an
insecticidal shampoo.

Consult your veterinarian. Your dog
may be suffering from an allergy or
skin infection.

These are probably ticks. Ask
your veterinarian to remove them;
partial removal can lead to
abscesses.

TAKING A DOG'S TEMPERATURE

A dog's normal temperature varies between 38° and 39°C (100° and 102°F) and it can be useful to check this if you are wondering if a veterinary appointment is necessary. Ask a helper to restrain and soothe the dog while you use a snub-nosed glass thermometer, the end greased with vegetable oil. Shake down the mercury, then lift the dog's tail and insert the thermometer slowly but firmly for about 2.5cm (1in) into the dog's rectum. Hold it in place for about half a minute, then remove and wipe before reading the temperature.

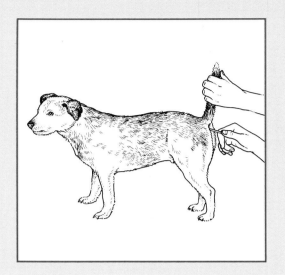

GIVING A PILL

You may be able to camouflage the pill in a piece of chocolate, meat or cheese but dogs are very good at detecting unwelcome additions to food and may well spit it out immediately. If this is the case, then have a favourite tidbit ready while you follow these steps:

1 Place your left hand over the dog's muzzle and raise its head slightly, meanwhile pressing its jaws gently with your thumb and index finger.

2 Put your thumb into the space behind the long canine tooth and press gently on the roof of the mouth, so that the dog keeps its mouth open.

3 With the right hand, place the pill at the base of the dog's tongue.

4 Close the dog's mouth, then hold it closed and stroke the dog's throat to encourage it to swallow. It it does so, give the tidbit and praise it.

5 If it refuses to swallow, hold the tidbit close to its nose. Its mouth will water and force it to swallow. Give it both tidbit and praise.

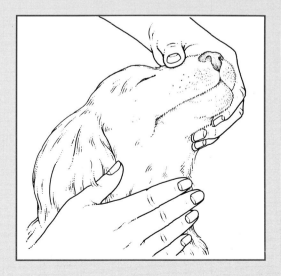

IMPROVISING A MUZZLE

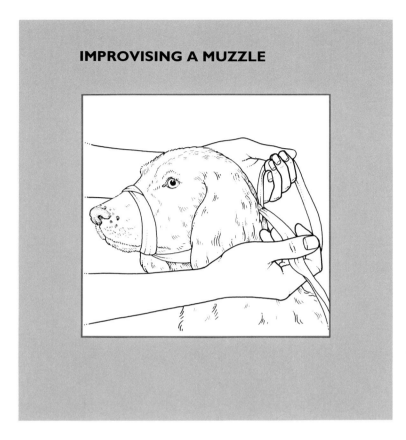

MAKING THE MOST OF YOUR VETERINARIAN

When choosing a veterinarian, ask around among local dog owners – or, better still, dog breeders – to find the most highly-rated practitioner in the area. When you first acquire your dog, take it along for a check-up whether it needs vaccinations or not. The veterinarian will then know your dog and have a record of its past history before you have to hasten to the surgery with a problem. Check whether he or she is willing to make housecalls if necessary and what arrangements are made for 24 hour emergency cover.

When you take your dog along for treatment, make a note of any symptoms and how long they have lasted so far. Be precise about any change in eating, drinking or toilet habits, any change in the appearance of faeces, or any alterations in behaviour. The more details the veterinarian has to work on, the more accurate his diagnosis is likely to be.

If you want to change your veterinarian, either because you move house or because you are not satisfied with the service

LEFT: *A dog which has been well looked after gives pleasure for many years.*

you get, it is in your dog's interest to notify your current practice. You do not need to give any explanation; simply ask for your dog's records to be transferred to your new veterinarian.

RESTRAINING A DOG

Your veterinarian will usually want the dog on a table for examination and you should be prepared to restrain it throughout. With a small dog, hold it by the scruff of the neck, including the collar, with your other hand behind the forelegs. With a large dog, put your arm around the throat, so that the dog's head is resting on your elbow. Put your other arm around its body and hold one of its front legs. Lean forwards, so that your body is touching the dog's shoulders.

If your dog is frightened or in pain it may try to bite to defend itself, so it is safer to use an improvised muzzle before attempting to examine or lift it, or to dress a wound. In the surgery a bandage is the best answer but at home you could use a nylon stocking or a tie. Make the fabric into a large loop, slip it over the dog's muzzle and tie a half knot – not too tightly – on the top of its nose. Loop the fabric again and knot it again under the jaws. Cross over the ends, bring them round the neck and tie them securely in a bow behind the ears.

NURSING A SICK DOG

The sick dog's bed should be in a quiet, warm, well-ventilated place without draughts. A well-wrapped hot water bottle, filled with warm water and re-filled frequently will help to keep it snug. Plenty of layers of newspaper topped with old towels or sweaters will make comfortable, disposable bedding which can be changed as often as necessary.

The dog may be off its food, so tempt it with small, frequent meals of cooked white fish or poultry or scrambled egg. Warm the food to blood temperature and feed by hand if necessary. Your dog will not starve if it is unable to eat for a time but dehydration can be a danger, particularly if it is vomiting or has diarrhoea. Your veterinarian may advise liquidized meals, fish or meat juices or a glucose and water mixture, which can be fed through a syringe if the dog will not drink. If you have to use a syringe, put your left hand over the dog's muzzle and raise its head slightly, as you would to give a pill, and part the jaws just enough to insert the syringe between the canine tooth and the molar on the right side. Pump the liquid through a little at a time, pausing to give the dog a chance to swallow and don't tilt

ADMINISTERING EAR DROPS

Lift the flap of the ear (on long-eared dogs) and use damp cotton wool to clean away any visible dirt or wax but do not poke around in the ear canal. Tilt the head slightly sideways and hold it still. Put the nozzle of the bottle just inside the ear and administer the correct number of drops. Continue to hold the head steady, drop the ear flap and gently massage the ear. Once the drops have had the chance to penetrate, clean away any excess fluid. Never administer ear drops without veterinary advice.

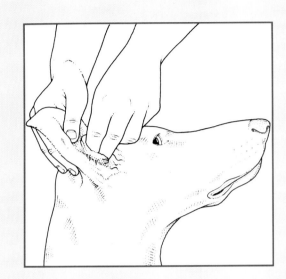

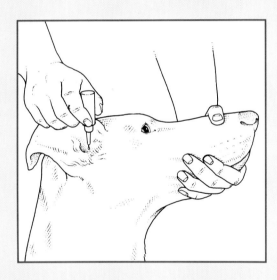

the dog's head too far back or the liquid may go down the 'wrong way' and cause choking.

While the dog is ill, clean its face regularly by wiping away any discharge from around the eyes, nose and mouth, using a clean pad of dampened cotton wool for each area. If it suffers from diarrhoea, you will need to clean its rear end as well.

When the dog needs to go outside, take it out for the shortest possible time. If it is too ill to walk, carry it out wrapped in a blanket and put it down in the appropriate place. A small dog can be encouraged to use a cat's litter tray, particularly if it is filled with garden soil to remind it of outdoor smells, and in the worst case, put plenty of newspaper in one corner of a room that can be easily disinfected and put the dog on that at the appropriate times. Accept any messes without scolding; your dog will probably be as depressed about them as you are.

EMERGENCY ACTION

Following an accident or emergency, you will need to take your dog to the veterinarian as quickly as possible, but administering the right first aid on the spot could save its life. An injured dog may snap, so always consider improvising a muzzle before you take any action to help a conscious dog. Give the dog nothing to eat or drink in case it needs as anaesthetic later.

APPLYING EYE DROPS/OINTMENT

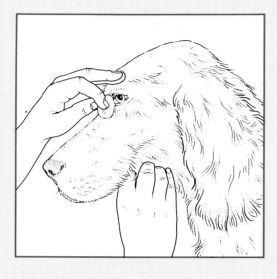

Hold the dog's head steady for a few seconds so that it does not shake out the drops. Follow the same procedure when applying ointment, then pull down the lower eyelid and squeeze out a small amount of ointment onto the inside of the lid. Hold the eye closed for a few seconds.

First, clean away any discharge from around the eye, then ask a helper to restrain the dog's head.

Hold the eye open, bring the hand holding the eye dropper from above and behind, so that the dog does not wince away from it, and squeeze in the drops.

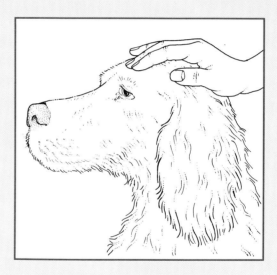

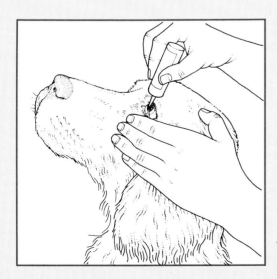

Take care not to touch the eye with dropper or tube. Never use human eye medicines or use anything prescribed for another animal.

Resuscitation

Only attempt resuscitation if you have satisfied yourself that the dog's breathing or heart has stopped and your actions are essential to save the dog's life, as you risk causing further damage to an injured animal. Whenever possible, see that someone telephones the veterinarian while you attempt resuscitation.

If the dog has stopped breathing, test for a heartbeat with your fingertips on the left side of the chest just behind the elbow, or by putting your ear against the chest. If there is a heartbeat, however faint, then loosen the dog's collar and give artificial respiration. Remove any obstruction from the mouth, pull the tongue forwards and stretch out the neck. Then place both hands on the left-hand side of the chest and press down firmly. Release immediately, then repeat every five seconds. Keep trying for as long as the heart is beating. If the dog appears to have chest injuries, try mouth-to-mouth resuscitation instead. Clear the mouth as before, then cup your hands over the dog's nose, keeping its jaws closed, and breathe hard into it nostrils. Wait for two seconds, then repeat and continue as long as necessary.

If the heart stops, give cardiac massage by placing one hand on top of the other on the dog's chest - after clearing the airways and pulling forward the tongue, as above. Firmly press both hands downwards and forwards towards the head. Be careful not to use too much force with a small dog, but large dogs will require vigorous pressure. Repeat the heart massage six times at one-second intervals, then alternate with mouth-to-mouth resuscitation and continue.

MOVING AN INJURED DOG

When a dog has been injured in a road accident, it will have to be moved as quickly as possible even though, in other circumstances, it would be better to leave it where it is until you know the extent of its injuries. If you have help - with a large dog, three people will be better than two - lift the dog's body onto a coat or blanket, keeping it as flat as possible by supporting the head, back and pelvis.

If you have to manage alone, lay the blanket right up to the dog's back then move its body one section at a time and pull the blanket along the ground until you reach a safe place and can call assistance. Then two people can lift the blanket with a hand at each corner, keeping it taut. If possible, have a third person supporting the back of a medium-to-large dog.

FIRST-AID KIT

Thermometer
Blunt-ended scissors
Tweezers
Gauze pads
Cotton wool
Cotton wool buds
Bandages (various widths)
Antiseptic cream (as recommended by your veterinarian)
Petroleum jelly

BLEEDING

A minor injury can be cleaned with a dampened cotton wool pad. Any matted hair should then be trimmed away with blunt-ended scissors and a mild antiseptic applied. If a wound is bleeding profusely, hold a gauze pad soaked in cold water firmly over it. If the blood soaks through, apply more dressings on top but do not remove the first one. Then bandage firmly over the dressings, taking care not to restrict the circulation and take the dog to the veterinarian. Don't use a tourniquet; you are likely to do more harm than good.

DROWNING

Dogs like to swim and the result is, unfortunately, that they sometimes get into trouble. If you find yourself fishing a drowned dog out of the water, you will need to take speedy action. Try to get a small dog breathing again by picking it up by the back legs and shaking it gently to get the water out of its lungs. If this does not re-start breathing, lie the dog on its side and begin artificial respiration, as above. Lay a large dog on its side immediately, with its body higher than its head and lift its back end as high as you can. After half a minute, begin artificial respiration.

CHOKING

If your dog gets a piece of bone or splinter of wood stuck in its mouth or throat, you may be able to remove it yourself with the aid of tweezers. Ask a helper to restrain the dog *(see page 87)*, then open its mouth, as above. If you can't see the foreign body, or it seems stuck fast don't poke about, as you may do even more damage. The next step is to rush your dog to the veterinarian immediately.

ARTIFICIAL RESPIRATION

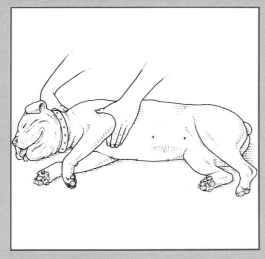

1 Test for a heartbeat on the left side of the chest below the elbow.

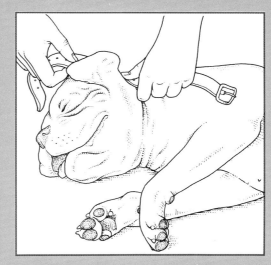

2 If there is a heartbeat, remove the collar and give artificial respiration.

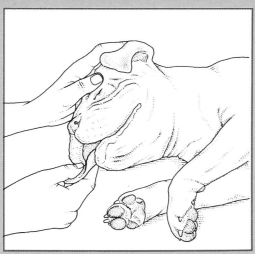

3 Stretch out the neck and pull the tongue forward.

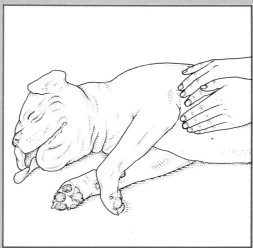

4 Place hands on left side of chest. Press firmly, release immediately and repeat every 5 seconds.

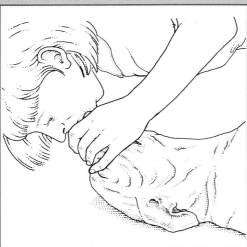

Mouth-to-mouth resuscitation is better for dogs with chest injuries (see page 90).

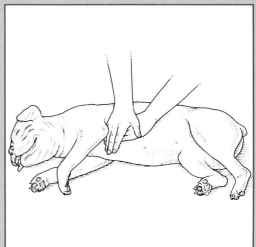

If the heart stops, give cardiac massage (see page 90).

MOVING AN INJURED DOG

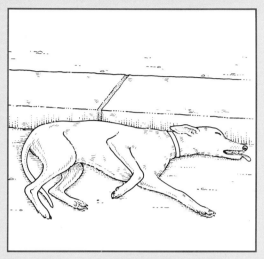

1 The dog lies injured at the side of the road.

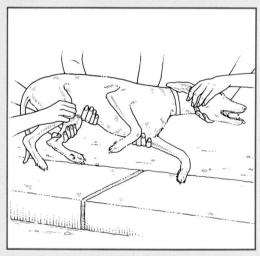

2 Three people are required to lift a large dog onto a coat or blanket.

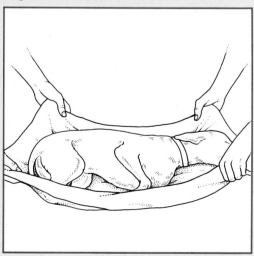

3 Two people are required to carry the dog gently to safety.

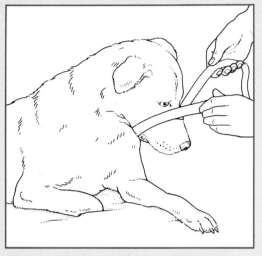

4 If the dog is conscious and in pain, it is sensible to improvise a muzzle *(see page 87)*.

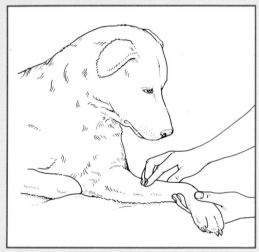

5 Gently check the dog's body to assess injured areas.

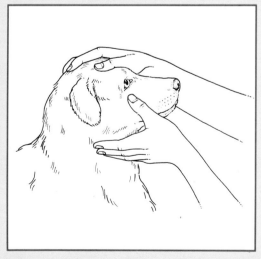

6 Pull back the dog's eyelids gently, to assess the condition of the pupils.

STINGS

In most cases of stings, an ice pack applied to the swelling is all that is needed, though a vinegar solution applied to a wasp sting can be helpful. If you see a bee sting embedded in the dog's flesh, remove it with tweezers. Few dogs have serious allergic reactions to stings but swellings in the mouth can impede breathing so take a veterinarian's advice.

HEATSTROKE

Many dogs suffer heatstroke in hot weather, especially if they have been left confined in cars. The symptoms are heavy panting, frothing at the mouth and possibly vomiting. First clear the dog's mouth of frothy saliva and sponge its face with cold water, then put wet towels over its body and pour on cold water as they warm up.

FISH HOOK IN THE MOUTH

One of the regular hazards of being a dog living near the coast or walking on river banks seems to be fish hooks caught in the mouth. If you see a piece of line hanging from the dog's mouth,

BELOW: *Dogs develop their own ways of keeping cool in hot weather.*

RESCUING A DROWNED DOG

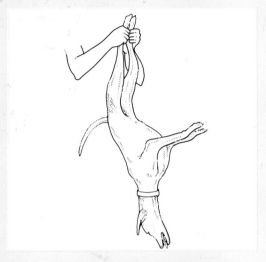

Pick up the dog by its hind legs and shake it gently.

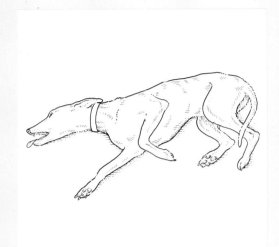

Lie the dog on its side and begin artificial respiration *(see page 91).*

don't pull on it as the hook will only bed in more tightly. Instead, ask a helper to restrain the dog and open its mouth. If you can see the hook clearly you may be able to release it by easing it forward and cutting off the barbed tip with a pair of pliers, then removing the rest as smoothly as possible. If you cannot see the hook, take the dog to the veterinarian. Sometimes dogs swallow fish hooks completely and, in such cases, it may be necessary to take X-rays and even surgery may be required.

BURNS AND SCALDS

If your dog suffers a burn or scald, apply cold water gently but thoroughly to the area or use an ice pack made from ice cubes sealed in a plastic bag, or a packet of frozen peas wrapped in a clean cloth. Afterwards you can apply petroleum jelly to a minor burn but anything more serious should have veterinary attention. Wash any chemical from your dog's coat with plenty of clean water and contact the veterinarian.

FIRST AID ON A BURN

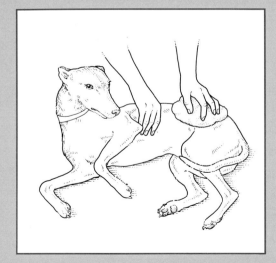

Gently apply an ice pack to the affected area.

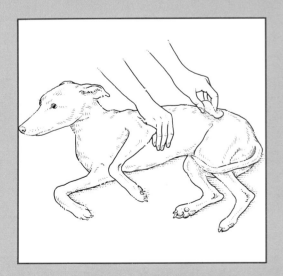

Provided the burn is minor, apply petroleum jelly.

HEALTH DANGERS FROM DOGS

The most serious and frightening of the diseases that can spread from dogs to humans is rabies, which is transmitted in the saliva of an infected animal. Great Britain is rabies-free but in many countries the disease is carried by wild animals and passed on to domestic pets. If you are bitten by a dog, or any other animal, in a country where rabies is endemic, wash the wound with alcohol and go straight to the doctor.

Owners who do not worm their dogs are taking risks with the health of their own and other people's children. Toxocara roundworm larvae are excreted by dogs and become infectious later. Children between the ages of 18 months and three years who ingest dog-soiled earth are most susceptible to toxocariasis, which can cause blindness. This is a rare condition but it is wise to take precautions: teach children to wash their hands after playing with dogs and do not let them play in areas where dogs defecate. As far as your own dog is concerned, the best precaution is regular worming, but of course it is common sense to keep your children away from the area the dog uses as a toilet.

Always clear up after your own dog. If you dislike carrying a 'pooper-scooper' then take along a plastic bag you can use on your hand like a glove. Pick up the 'nasties' then fold the bag inside out to enclose them. Not scooping is anti-social and, very often, against the law.

INSURANCE

Most veterinary surgeries have pamphlets advertising insurance schemes for dogs. Different companies offer varying benefits, including covering the costs of veterinary treatment, reimbursement if your dog is lost or stolen, cover for kennel fees if you are hospitalized, accidental death payments and damages payable to third parties. Veterinary costs can be very high and if you fear that you might not be able to meet the bills if your dog becomes ill or is injured, then insurance is a good idea. On the other hand, it will cost you many hundreds of pounds over the years and the small print usually explains that you have to meet the first £25 or so (at current prices) of every claim for veterinary treatment. If you do decide to take insurance, decide exactly what cover you want: if you are only interested in covering veterinary bills, take a simple, no frills policy without extra benefits and with lower premiums.

ABOVE: *A much-loved member of the family, this shaggy old English sheepdog repays its owner's care many times over.*

INDEX